W9-ALN-115

DISCARD

JOURNEY TO AMERICA

Chantrea Conway's Story

A Voyage from Cambodia in 1975

JOURNEY TO AMERICA

Chantrea Conway's Story

A Voyage from Cambodia in 1975

CLARE PASTORE

BERKLEY JAM BOOKS, NEW YORK

JOURNEY TO AMERICA: CHANTREA CONWAY'S STORY:
A VOYAGE FROM CAMBODIA IN 1975

A Berkley Jam Book / published by arrangement with
the author

PRINTING HISTORY
Berkley Jam edition / May 2001

The Penguin Putnam Inc. World Wide Web site address is
www.penguinputnam.com

ISBN: 0-425-17889-7

BERKLEY JAM BOOKS®
Berkley Jam Books are published by The Berkley Publishing Group,
a division of Penguin Putnam Inc.,
375 Hudson Street, New York, New York 10014.
BERKLEY JAM and its logo
are trademarks belonging to Penguin Putnam Inc.

PRINTED IN THE UNITED STATES OF AMERICA

10 9 8 7 6 5 4 3 2 1

Chapter One

CHANTREA Conway and her mother stood at the front door of their apartment building in Phnom Penh, Cambodia, hugging Chantrea's father good-bye as he left for a business trip. He was so tall that they had to stand on the first step to look into his hazel eyes. Chantrea leaned forward to kiss him once again, laughing as his mustache tickled her in spite of the sadness she felt.

"That feels just like a caterpillar," Chantrea said.

"Your grandmother says it makes me look like a barbarian," her father replied. "What do you think?"

"I think it's nice," Chantrea told him, and sighed. "Father, will you be gone long this time?"

"Not more than a few days," he assured her. "Don't be sad, Chantrea. You should be used to my trips by now, and I always bring you back a surprise, dont I?"

"Yes, but I wish I could go with you." Chantrea

1

sighed. Chantrea knew she was too old to be making such a fuss, but she always hated it when her father had to leave on his trips.

"We'll travel together this summer to America," he reminded her. "You'll see your American grandparents again. But I have to go on this trip alone to Siem Reap."

Chantrea nodded. It would be fun to visit America, to see relatives she hadn't seen for five years. But that wasn't her first thought right now.

She bit her lip. "Father, there is so much fighting in our country. It scares me."

"I'll be careful, Chantrea," he said. "I promise."

Seth Conway was a photographer who worked for a magazine called *American World View*. He did most of his work here in Cambodia, and sent his photographs overseas to the magazine's headquarters in Columbus, Ohio. Pride swelled in Chantrea each time she saw one of his pictures. But she still wished he did not have to go away so often to take them.

Now Chantrea's mother spoke. While Father had used English, Mother used Khmer. Chantrea had grown up hearing two languages, and now she could easily speak and read both Khmer, the official language of her country, and English.

"Chantrea, you know it is your father's job. It is money for food and shelter many others do not have."

Dara Conway's strong voice did not match her petite frame. She barely stood as tall as Father's shoulder. At thirteen, Chantrea was already two inches taller than her mother. Father had said she'd be a tall woman when she grew up, just like most of her American relatives. Like her mother, Chantrea was blessed with shining black hair, but unlike her mother, Chantrea's dark brown eyes were just slightly rounded instead of almond-shaped. She knew she was pretty, but she didn't think she would ever be as beautiful as her mother. Mother had hair like black silk and skin like fresh cream. Chantrea thought she was as lovely as a porcelain figurine.

Dara laid a delicate, long-fingered hand against her husband's cheek.

"Still, I wish you would return quickly, Seth," she said. A look of worry passed briefly over her lovely face, then vanished.

"I'll be back before you know it," he said with a reassuring smile. He leaned forward to give his wife one last kiss. Then he patted Chantrea's shoulder. "See you in a few days, honey."

He strode away, climbed into a little blue Volkswagen Beetle and started the engine.

"Good-bye, Father," Chantrea called in Khmer.

"Good-bye," he called back in English as he pulled away from the curb. He had to move slowly, because the street was crowded with people. Just before he turned the corner, he poked his hand out the window for a final wave. His steel watchband glistened under the hot Cambodian sun.

"We should go inside, Chantrea," her mother said, and after one last look at the little car driving away, Chantrea followed her mother back to their apartment.

Her mother did not speak of her worry or sadness, but Chantrea knew what she felt. There was so much to fear in Cambodia these days. When Chantrea was little,

3

a man named Norodom Sihanouk had been ruler. Then, in 1970, General Lon Nol overthrew his regime and took over the country. He hated the Cambodian Communists, known as the Khmer Rouge. Civil war was tearing the country apart. Chantrea often heard about cities being bombed. The place Father had gone had been under attack recently, and she prayed that he would be safe. Even more frightening was the possibility that Phnom Penh would also become a target of the Khmer Rouge bombers.

But there were a lot of people who felt they were safe in Cambodia's capital city, for countless refugees of the civil war had poured into the city from other towns. A few years ago Chantrea had been able to run all the way to her grandparents' house, just outside the city. Now her way was blocked by crowds of homeless people.

As they walked up the stairs to their apartment, her mother put her arm around Chantrea and announced, "We will make *ansamcheks* and bring them to your grandparents."

Chantrea was glad to go back into their cool apartment. It was the hottest part of the day, and people outside crowded into what little patches of shade they could find. The afternoon sun in Cambodia was so hot that few did more than rest until it passed. Mother had always made desserts to relax, and Chantrea loved to help her.

Mother turned on the radio, and the announcer told of the latest events of the civil war. Quickly, Mother turned the dial until she found soft, pleasant music.

"Such news is not good for children," she mumbled, as if Chantrea couldn't hear her.

Chantrea began to peel bananas to make a filling for the rice cakes, but she couldn't remain silent.

"The soldiers fight so much," Chantrea said. "I hate it. I don't like Father out there."

Mother said nothing. She looked out the window, as if she could see the road where Father drove his little Volkswagen Beetle. Chantrea knew that it hurt her mother to talk about the danger Father faced each time he went on an assignment in their war-torn country. She bit her lip to silence herself, and said nothing more as they worked on the *ansamcheks*. Chantrea couldn't wait to taste the delicious rice cakes, with their sweet banana filling.

Two more hours passed before it was cool enough to walk to the house where Chantrea's grandparents lived. Chantrea was impatient to see them. Grandfather Meng was so sweet and kind, and he always knew how to make Chantrea laugh. He knew magic tricks, and he carved little animals and beads for necklaces for her from teak. Grandfather had been a schoolteacher, and Chantrea thought he was the smartest man in the world next to her own father. Grandmother was stern and took no nonsense, but she knew wonderful stories and sewed the most beautiful clothes for Chantrea. Today, Chantrea had traded her favorite jeans and T-shirt for a *sampot* her grandmother had made. Grandmother did not approve of Western-style dress. Out of respect, Chantrea always wore the knee-length tunic and pants when she went to visit her grandparents. She did not mind, though. Grandmother's embroidery was admired by everyone who saw it.

Grandfather had a little flower garden, where he grew beautiful orchids to sell to tourists. Today he picked two and gave one to Chantrea and one to her mother.

"Hello, Father." Chantrea's mother made a respectful bow as part of her greeting.

Meng bowed to his daughter in return. Chantrea thought Grandfather was a very handsome man, with dark, smiling eyes and thick black hair that was touched with just a little bit of gray near his eyes.

"Good evening, Grandfather," Chantrea said, and pressed her hands together and made her own little bow of respect.

"Hello, Chantrea," he replied in English. "What's happening?"

Chantrea smiled. Grandfather was just a few years older than Father, and the two men liked each other a lot. Father had taught Meng several modern American expressions and Meng loved to use them.

"Father has gone to Siem Reap," Chantrea told him.

Grandfather nodded. "His work takes him to many places."

He led his daughter and granddaughter into the little house where he and his wife had lived since his retirement. It was made of bamboo, with a palm thatched roof. Grandmother always kept the inside neatly swept and dusted. Most of the furniture was of simple Cambodian design, but Grandfather's prized possession was a big rolltop desk Father had had sent over from America for him. His favorite books, written in Khmer, Chinese, English, or French, sat between two ornate dragon bookends on the desktop.

Chantrea and her mother greeted Grandmother. The older woman stood at a table near the window as she wrapped fish in spinach leaves. She nodded to them and went back to her work. It made Chantrea think of her grandmother in America, who also liked to cook. She thought about the trip they would take there in a few months, to a place called "Ohio" and wondered how different it would be from her memories. She had only been seven when she last went.

Chantrea had traveled to America three times in her life. Once, she was only a little baby and the second time she was just four. Father took her to Ohio when she was seven, old enough to remember some of the things that happened there. Grandma Laura and Grandpa Joey were wonderful to her and showed her a lot of love. But Chantrea was also old enough to see that her grandparents sometimes acted a little strangely around Mother. She had a very vivid memory of hearing her mother crying to her father, "They don't like me!" And Father insisted that they did, they just had to "get to know her." Chantrea didn't know it then, but understood now that they had not been happy about a marriage between their son and a Cambodian woman. Would they still act that way when the family went to visit this summer? Chantrea hoped not. She never wanted anything to make her mother cry. She hoped Grandma Laura and Grandpa Joey would be as kind to Mother as her Cambodian grandparents were to their American son-in-law.

"What are you thinking of, Chantrea?" Grandfather asked.

"My American grandparents," Chantrea replied. "We

7

are going to visit them this summer, and my uncle and cousins, too. I can't wait to go to America."

Uncle Bill's son had only been a baby, but cousin Kathy was just a little older than Chantrea. She had been very nice and the two girls had had a lot of fun together. Kathy hadn't seemed to mind at all that her aunt Dara was Cambodian.

Chantrea worried again about how they would treat Mother.

"I wish you could go with us," she said to her grandparents.

Grandmother made a *hmmph* noise. Her thick black hair rustled against her small shoulders as she shrugged.

"My home is good enough for me," she said. "I never want to leave Cambodia."

"I think I might like it in America," Grandfather said. "At least, for a visit."

They soon sat down to a delicious meal of prawn soup, rice, mixed greens, and fish. Everyone enjoyed the *ansamcheks*, and Grandmother said that Dara and Chantrea did a fine job with the dessert.

Later, the adults sat outside to drink their tea. Chantrea knelt by Grandfather's goldfish pond and watched the fish. Their scales shone like gold in the moonlight. She listened silently to the adults talk. Mother truly was worried about the news she'd heard about the civil war. Grandfather, usually so happy after a good meal, spoke in hushed tones.

"This war must end soon," he said, "or it will destroy us completely."

"Tomorrow," Grandmother said, "we will go to the *wat*

and make an offering to our ancestors for their continued protection."

Chantrea liked to visit the *wat*. The Buddhist temple was so beautiful and so peaceful. She did not have school the next day, so she was able to join her mother and grandparents. They each took turns before the altar of Buddha. It was richly decorated with statues, candles, and flowers. When it was her turn, Chantrea closed her eyes and prayed:

"Buddha, keep my father safe and make the soldiers stay away from our city. Bring peace to our country."

On the way home, they passed a procession of monks on the road. Grandmother gave the leader a small bundle. Chantrea knew it was filled with bread and vegetables, for the monks relied on the kindness of others for their food. They looked so peaceful that she wished she could be like them, free of fear and worry.

———

CHANTREA'S father called two days later, and told his family that he had been asked to go on to Battambang. Chantrea was sad when he told her he wouldn't be home for at least another week.

"Don't worry, Chantrea," her father said. "It will go by quickly. And when I come back, I'll have that surprise I promised you."

Now Chantrea's spirits lifted. She loved surprises.

"What is it, Father?" she asked excitedly.

He laughed. "You know I can't tell you that, or it wouldn't be a surprise. Give the phone back to your mom now, okay? I love you, sweetheart."

"Love you, too," Chantrea said, and gave the receiver to her mother.

She listened to her mother's end of the phone conversation as she ate a lunch of warm French bread and salad her mother had bought at the market that morning. Mother sounded worried. Several times she said, "I understand." Chantrea wished she could know what Father said, but Mother revealed nothing when she hung up the phone. Chantrea did not ask the questions that filled her mind. The answers were private between Mother and Father, and it would be disrespectful to pry.

"I have a headache," Mother said. "I think it is hotter today than it has ever been. The air is so thick, I almost wish the monsoons would start early and bring us relief."

She went into her bedroom and closed the door. Chantrea finished her lunch, then wandered outside to look for her friends. Kalliyan, Sothea, and Chantou sat under the shade of a breadfruit tree.

"Did you finish the math assignment we were given for the weekend?" Kalliyan asked.

"I haven't even started it," Chantrea replied. "My father usually helps me with that, but I guess I'll have to do it on my own this time. Perhaps I'll bring it to my grandfather." She sighed. "I wish my father would come home soon."

"*My* father says the Americans will invade our city one day," Sothea said, a look of disapproval on her round face. "They have already dropped bombs on our borders."

"My father says they chase the Vietnamese communists who hide there," Chantrea retorted.

"It is our people who are hurt," Sothea insisted.

"When the Americans attack our city, too, who will you be loyal to then, Mok Chantrea?"

"My name is Chantrea Conway," Chantrea insisted. She didn't want to fight with her friends but this was not the first time they had argued about her name. She held onto her temper with effort.

"Your *American* name," Sothea said scornfully, emphasizing "American" as if it were a dirty word. "And it sounds strange to hear your given name first! Why don't they give the family name first, as we do in Cambodia?"

"I don't know," Chantrea said with a shrug. "It's just a different way."

"I think it would be fun to have two names," Kalliyan said, obviously trying to keep peace between her friends. "One Cambodian name, with the family name first, and one American name with your given name at the front."

Sothea gave Chantrea's thigh a poke. "Answer my question, Chantrea. Where is your loyalty?"

"I will be loyal to those I love," Chantrea told her angrily.

Chantou moved closer to Chantrea and put an arm over her shoulder. She gave Sothea a defiant look.

"Leave her alone," she said. "Can't you see she is lonely for her father?"

Chantrea smiled at her. "Father is going to bring me a surprise."

"You are lucky," Kalliyan said. "Your father always brings you the nicest presents."

"If it's candy," Chantou asked, "will you share?"

Chantrea laughed. "Of course! I'll even share with you, Sothea, even though you don't like Americans."

11

Sothea snorted and got up to stomp away.

"She sounds like an old water buffalo when she does that," Kalliyan remarked.

All the girls giggled. They enjoyed another hour of conversation in spite of the heat, and when Chantrea heard her mother call, she went inside reluctantly.

"Is your headache better?" she asked.

"A little," Mother said, "now that the sun is going down. Chantrea, take out the bowls for soup. I was able to find a little pork at the market today."

In the past few months the market, which had once overflowed with abundance, had become emptier and emptier. Food supplies were scarce because of the fighting, and meat was the hardest to get. Chantrea considered herself very lucky as she ate her pork and rice soup, flavored with ginger and little pieces of vegetables. When she went to bed that night, she thanked Buddha for the meal, and asked him once again to watch over Father.

Chapter Two

CHANTREA'S alarm clock woke her for school the next morning. She pulled on her favorite comfortable jeans and a T-shirt with a picture of an American rock group called The Eagles on it. Father had played their music for her, and she liked it. She laughed softly to herself, and thought of the day she'd sung a few lines for Grandfather. Grandmother, who thought such music was vulgar, had been very upset. She could be so very old-fashioned, Chantrea thought.

After breakfast, she kissed Mother good-bye and headed to her school. She met Kalliyan along the way. As they turned a corner, a teenaged boy ran up to them.

"The war is over! The war is over!" he cried.

"What do you mean?" Chantrea asked.

"The fighting is done!" the boy said, as a big grin spread across his face. "Cambodia is finally at peace!"

13

Chantrea looked at Kalliyan. "What is today's date?"

"April 17th," Kalliyan said with a smile.

Chantrea said the date over and over in her mind: April 17th, the day peace came to Cambodia at last. Both girls started to run by people who crowded into the streets. Everyone danced and shouted with joy. At their school, they were told to go home. School was closed for the day to celebrate!

Army trucks rumbled through the streets. When Chantrea saw their red flags, she felt uneasy for just a moment. The Khmer Rouge had been the victors. Father hadn't liked them. He said they were dangerous. But she pushed her worries away. After so many years of fighting, did it matter who the winner was, as long as there was peace?

She said good-bye to Kalliyan and ran back to her apartment again. She found Mother at a window, gazing down at the crowds in the streets.

"*La paix*, Mother!" Chantrea cried in French, just like some of the people in the streets. "Peace, at last! It's wonderful!"

Mother turned to her, worry in her eyes. "Is it, Chantrea? I can't help but feel strange about this."

Chantrea remembered the moments she'd felt uneasy, too.

"Why, Mother?"

Mother held out an arm and Chantrea went to stand next to her.

"Look at the Khmer Rouge soldiers," Mother said. "What do you see?"

Chantrea studied their faces—some of them no more

14

than boys—and in a moment she knew at once why she'd felt troubled earlier. Despite all the people who shouted and sang, the soldiers did not smile. Their faces were cold, stern. They did not look like happy victors, but like men with a grave and important mission ahead of them.

"What does it mean, Mother?" Chantrea asked, a feeling of dread building inside her.

"I don't know, Chantrea," Mother said. "But I don't like it. How I wish your Father were here. He would know what to do."

She stepped away from the window and ordered her daughter to do the same. Mother prayed at her little altar to Buddha while Chantrea sat in her room and watched the celebration below. A short time later, Mother knocked at her door and told her to join her for lunch.

They had barely finished their bowls of rice when someone pounded at the door. It was a neighbor, Seng Varin.

"We are under attack! We are under attack!" he cried.

"What do you mean?" Mother demanded.

Through the open window, Chantrea heard someone scream in terror.

Varin took a deep breath. "The Americans are on the way with their jets and bombs! We have to evacuate, or we'll all die!"

"That can't be true!" Chantrea cried.

"Everyone must evacuate!" Varin insisted and ran to knock on someone else's door.

Chantrea turned to her mother. "The Americans won't really bomb us, will they? Not Father's people?"

"I don't know." Her mother shook her head. "I don't believe that. Something is very wrong here."

She dashed to the window, face tight with fear, Chantrea by her side. Chantrea saw the streets fill up as her neighbors poured out of their buildings. Shouts of anger against Americans filled the air. She prayed that her father was safe. Khmer Rouge soldiers were everywhere, guns ready. If they want to save us, Chantrea wondered, why do they point guns at everyone?

Her mother took Chantrea by the shoulders and turned her around. "Chantrea, your father thought there might be some bad trouble, because you are part American. We have to hurry to your grandparents' house so that you can hide, until we are certain what is happening."

"Hide?" Chantrea's voice was a squeak. "Why do I have to hide? I didn't do anything wrong!"

But Mother said no more. She did not stop to let Chantrea pack a few things. She did not even give her time to change from her jeans into a *sampot*. She simply pulled her by the hand and hurried out the back of the apartment building. They stayed in alleyways and back streets as they made their way to the outskirts of the city. By the time they reached Grandfather's house, Chantrea was in tears. She did not understand what was happening, and the fear inside grew and grew.

"You will be safe here," her mother said, and hugged her tight.

"Mother, tell me why I have to hide!"

"The Khmer Rouge hate all foreigners," Mother said. "I think they hate the Americans and the Vietnamese

16

most. If they learn your father is American they'll . . .
they'll . . ."

Mother burst into tears and Grandfather put his arm
around her small shoulders. Chantrea knew at once that
the Khmer Rouge would kill her simply because she was
half-American. She felt icy all over, in spite of the morning
heat.

"You must go now, Dara," Grandfather said. "We will
meet at the *wat*, as soon as this is over. Look for us there."

"Yes, yes," Mother said, nodding frantically. "I love
you, Chantrea! We will be together very soon!"

Mother turned to run away.

"Why can't she stay here with us?" Chantrea asked,
panic-stricken as she watched her mother disappear in
the distance.

"Others will tell of her American husband," Grandfather explained, "and of her daughter. They might come
looking for you."

"Won't they find me here?" Chantrea cried.

Grandfather smiled at her. "Do you remember my
magic chest?"

One of Grandfather's many talents was magic, and
he had carved a magnificent teak chest for a "disappearing
lady" trick. Unless you knew exactly how to open it, you
would only find empty space inside.

"I will hide there?" Chantrea asked.

"Only for a little while, in case the soldiers come,"
Grandfather told her.

Chantrea climbed into the chest, and twisted her
body into a tiny compartment beneath its false bottom.
The chest was carved so intricately that when you looked

inside, you did not realize the bottom you saw was too high compared to the outside.

"Only a little while," Grandfather promised.

But hours passed as Chantrea hid. There were breathing holes in the carvings of dragons and plum blossoms, but she could not move an inch, not even to relieve her screaming muscles. She heard her grandparents speak in soft tones. Every so often, the bamboo shades would creak, as if one of them was looking out the window. At last, Grandfather opened the top.

"If they meant to look for you," he said, "they would have come by now. I think you might be safe."

Chantrea's arms and legs were numb, and it felt as if fire crept into her joints. She stretched like a cat.

"What about my mother?" she asked eagerly. "When can I see my mother?"

"You must stay here until she comes for you," Grandfather insisted. "We can take no chances."

Grandmother stood by a window. She lifted the bamboo shade and gazed outside for a long time.

"Meng, the roads are full of people," she said, gesturing for him to come and see.

Grandfather and Chantrea went to look with her—to Chantrea, the road crowded with people seemed like a snake with a thousand heads moving slowly along the distant highway. She could see spots of green and red that were the Khmer Rouge trucks and their communist flags.

"What are they doing, Grandfather?" she asked.

"I don't know," he admitted.

"It looks like everyone is leaving Phnom Penh," Grandmother said.

Chantrea backed away from the window and stared at her grandparents.

"Mother might be down there," she cried. "I have to find her!"

"No!" Grandmother said in a stern voice. "It is not safe! You will stay here."

Chantrea looked to Grandfather, but he only shook his head sadly.

"Why are there so many people down there?" Grandmother said. "Did the Khmer Rouge arrest them all?"

"It does not make sense," Grandfather replied. "If they wanted to evacuate us to save us from the bombs, why bring everyone out into the open?"

"You know they tell lies, Meng," Grandmother said.

Chantrea looked out the window again. To her horror, she saw an army truck rumbling up the road to her grandparents' house. Grandfather saw it, too.

"Quickly, Chantrea," he urged. "You must hide again."

Chantrea obeyed. A few minutes later, there was a knock at the door. A man shouted that everyone was to leave the area.

"Angkar wills it," he snapped. "It is for your safety, before the Americans strike."

Chantrea's heart seemed to stop beating for just a moment when she heard the angry way he said "Americans." It scared Chantrea to hear the word *Angkar*. Father had told her all about them. He had said they were a very cruel, special committee of the Khmer Rouge. Anyone who did not obey their strict rules was punished by death.

19

"We will pack our things and . . ." she heard Grandfather say.

"No, you will come now!" the soldier ordered. "You need nothing! All will be provided by Angkar!"

Chantrea heard footsteps shuffle across the floor, then the sound of the door as it slammed shut. She wanted to cry out, *"Don't leave me here!"* but she did not dare. She listened to the sound of the truck's engine as it pulled away. Then there was nothing but silence. She lay for a long, long time, frozen in terror. Where were Grandmother and Grandfather? What had happened to them?

"Please, help me," she whispered. "Mother, come and find me!"

But no one came. The house grew dark, and the magic box became so stuffy even the breathing holes did not help. She knew she had to get out. But what if someone waited out there, in the dark and silence? What if the first thing she saw was a cruel grinning face at the end of a rifle?

She could not stand it. She worked at the inner latches, in the way that Grandfather had taught her, and escaped from the box. Her arms and legs felt like stiff bamboo poles as she stumbled about in the darkness. At once, Chantrea realized she was all alone.

She opened the front door, and moonlight beamed into the little house. The road outside was dark, but she could still see flickering lights from trucks and jeeps in the distance. She turned around and looked at the house where her family had shared so many happy times. A pot of rice grew cold on the stove. Grandfather's teacup was still half-full. There was a shawl Grandmother had begun to embroider with silk thread. There was a book Grandfather had almost completed. Chantrea felt tears rise and bit her lip. She knew that neither the book, nor the shawl, would ever be finished.

"I have to find Mother," she told herself. Her voice sounded strangely loud in the empty room.

She left the little house and hurried back toward the city. She did not take the road, but ran along a shortcut she had known since she was a child. In the past months, she had always had to move aside for people who blocked her way. But today, there was no one at all.

When Chantrea entered the city, she could not believe what she saw. Every street was empty. There were no lights in the buildings, and no cars moved in the alleyways. She hurried to her own apartment, but there was no one there. Mother was gone, marching with that snake of people Chantrea had seen from Grandfather's window.

Chantrea's heart beat so loudly she was certain someone would hear it and come to get her. She left the building and hid in the shadows as she walked through the city. She thought of a book Father had shown her once, a book about the American West in the 1800s. There was a name for a town that was deserted like this. It took her a few moments to remember what it was.

"Ghost town," she whispered to the empty street. "Phnom Penh is a ghost town."

Chantrea suddenly felt more afraid than she ever had in her life. She wanted to be with people, no matter who they were. She wanted to find her mother.

She began to run toward the people who had marched along the highway. Although hours had passed since the evacuation orders were given, they moved so slowly that

21

Chantrea easily caught up to them. She kept to the shadows so the Khmer Rouge soldiers would not see her. As for the people themselves, they were too frightened and confused to notice a girl as she slipped in among them.

Chapter Three

THEY marched all night, thousands of frightened and confused people. From the youngest child to the oldest man, no one was allowed to stop and rest. The soldiers insisted they had to flee the Americans, but whispers soon began to pass through the crowd. Was it all a lie? Was it a trick to get them away from the city, out into the open country? But why? No one dared ask these questions out loud. They were too frightened by the sounds of gunshots that rang throughout the night.

Chantrea tried to find a familiar face in the crowd. But there were thousands of people in Phnom Penh, and she saw no one that she knew. Finally, toward the end of the second day, she spotted her friend Chantou's mother. She pushed her way through the crowd and took the woman by the arm.

"Duong Sitha," she said, "have you seen my mother and my grandparents?"

Sitha stared at her with wide eyes that were puffed and red. Chantrea knew the woman had been crying. Something grew cold and hard inside her stomach.

"Is Chantou here?" she asked softly.

Sitha shook her head slowly. "She tried to run. She tried to run away from the soldiers and they . . ."

Sitha lifted a hand and waved it briskly, as if she wanted to drive away the truth about her daughter. What had happened to Chantou? Chantrea was terrified to think the soldiers might have killed her friend, a girl of only thirteen years.

Someone jostled Chantrea, and Sitha was pushed ahead into the crowd. Chantrea knew it was no use following the woman. She heard her mumble, "She tried to run," over and over, until her voice was lost among the tears and moans of those around her.

For the next days, as Chantrea searched desperately in the crowd for her family, she often looked over her shoulder to see if a rifle was aimed in *her* direction.

Sometimes, the group was allowed to stop and rest for a few precious minutes. One early morning, as they waited for the soldiers to force them to march again, Chantrea looked up and down the road. Her heart jumped as she saw soldiers throw bodies into the backs of the trucks. She had heard gunshots all night, but had never really imagined so many would be killed. Who were they? Friends, neighbors? She felt sick to her stomach. Maybe Chantou's body was in one of the trucks right near her.

Chantrea shuddered, the thought too horrible to bear.

She began to weave her way toward the shade of the road-side trees. Many people were so worn out they simply sat down on the highway. The soldiers on the trucks stared at them with cold, flinty eyes, no pity in their expressions.

As if we are animals in a slaughterhouse, Chantrea thought. Her lips pressed together and her eyes narrowed. But she quickly erased her angry look when one soldier turned in her direction. She averted her gaze, and hoped he had not seen her face.

Someone grabbed her ankle. Chantrea almost screamed, but she bit her lip to stop the sound. In just a few days, she had learned not to draw attention to herself. When she looked down, however, she almost cried out again to see that Grandfather sat right there on the road. Grandmother was at his side. How small and frail she looked now, weakened by this forced march! Chantrea longed to embrace them both. She knew it was only by a miracle she had found them in this huge mass. But she did not dare. She could only sit with her back to Grandfather as if she did not know him.

She heard Grandmother cough. Hatred swelled her heart. How could the Khmer Rouge soldiers be so cruel? How could they see these honorable old men and women, people who deserved respect, suffer like this?

She glanced over at a nearby truck, where two guards sat with rifles across their laps. They laughed as they ate big pieces of French bread. Chantrea's mouth watered and she realized how hungry she was. They had been given very little food by the soldiers.

When the soldiers looked elsewhere, Chantrea leaned back toward her grandfather and whispered, "Mother?"

Now he did look at her, and she saw there were tears in his eyes. Chantrea's stomach tightened. She had never seen Grandfather cry.

"Dead," he said. "Shot by a soldier."

He turned away without another word.

"My mother . . . is dead?" There was a huge roaring noise in Chantrea's head, and for a moment she felt she couldn't breathe. "But . . ."

"Hush, Chantrea," Grandmother ordered. "If they hear you speak, they might ask questions. And if they learn you are an American . . ."

Chantrea wanted to scream, to get up and run to the truck and strike the soldiers who laughed as if nothing was wrong. But Grandmother was right. She only dared to look at them, and only as long as their heads were turned away.

You killed my mother! she cried out in her mind.

But when one of the soldiers started to turn her way, she quickly ducked her head. Silent tears ran down her cheeks. No one asked about them. Tears were common now.

Chantrea thought of her beautiful mother, who she would never see again. She closed her eyes and tried to remember a happier day. The picture that came to her mind was of a summer day when she was seven, almost six years ago. Father wanted to teach her and Mother baseball and how to play catch. How they laughed each time they missed the ball! Chantrea had actually grown quite good at catching the ball, but Mother never took to it. After that, Father played catch with Chantrea as much as possible. When they went to the park near their apartment building, they were sometimes joined by other fathers and children in a game of baseball. Father told her all about his favorite baseball team, the Cincinnati Reds, and promised he would take her to a ball game in America someday.

A ray of hope filled Chantrea, despite the horrors around her. Father! Surely he was still alive! He would soon come back here to save her and her grandparents. He would take them far away from here, far away from the Khmer Rouge and their guns . . .

"Get up!" a soldier yelled suddenly.

Rifles were pointed and more orders shouted. Wearily, weak from days of marching and from hunger, everyone obeyed. They did not dare do otherwise.

They marched on all morning, until the day grew so hot even the soldiers did not want to move. There were abandoned houses along the road, and a few people went inside to escape the intense heat. Grandfather spotted a large mango tree and directed his wife and granddaughter toward it.

"But they should not know I belong to you, Grandfather," Chantrea protested.

Grandfather wiped sweat from his forehead with the back of his hand.

"They will learn soon enough," he said. "We are family. We must help each other."

Grandmother stumbled and Chantrea quickly put an arm around her. She helped her to the shade of the tree.

"So thirsty," Grandmother said, her voice like a bamboo chopstick rubbed against tree bark. She sounded like a woman in her nineties instead of the fifty-three-year-old that she really was.

Chantrea looked around, and spotted a small stream nearby. It was muddy, but it was so hot she didn't care. She didn't have anything to put the water into, so she cupped her hands and carried water back to her grandparents as carefully as she could. She tilted her hands toward Grandmother's lips. When Grandmother finished, Chantrea went back to get some water for herself. Grandfather was already at the stream, with many others, eagerly drinking the muddy water.

Chantrea barely got a sip into her throat when a gunshot made her, and the others, jump back. They were called to march again. By now, some of the sicker people crawled on the hot roadway. Chantrea saw now that even the hospitals had been emptied, and spotted a few wheelchairs and hospital beds in the throng. But the Khmer Rouge soldiers did not care. At that very moment, she realized that this evacuation was nothing more than a trick to empty the city. But where were they going? No one would say.

The march continued for days. Chantrea's sandal straps cut into her feet and made blisters on her skin. She didn't dare remove them, though. The road was littered with debris, and she was afraid she might step on something. The soldiers refused to help those who were truly sick or injured. There would be nothing she could do if a wound became infected.

As the days passed, she saw many people collapse in the heat. The soldiers forced some of them to get up and move again. Those who could not were left to die by the roadside, even though any one of the trucks that pushed through the crowds could easily have taken them to shelter.

There were two things that helped Chantrea get through those days. One was the thought that her father was certainly on his way to find her. The other was a little picture she had in the pocket of her jeans. It was taken when Mother and Father married. Whenever she thought it was safe, she took it out and gazed at it. It was Mother and Father's wedding picture. They looked so beautiful in traditional Cambodian costume. Father was so handsome in a white tunic embroidered with fine gold thread. And Mother was as pretty as a flower in a sarong of pink, yellow, and gold. She wore bangles on her bare arms of gold and teak, and sprigs of tropical blossoms were tucked into her dark hair.

She wished she had more pictures. It would be nice to have the one her grandma Laura had sent her from Ohio, a family portrait with her grandparents and cousins in front of a big Christmas tree. Or maybe the one of her cousin Kathy that had been taken at her school. Sometimes, as she lay on the ground in the sultry heat of the night, she wondered what her cousin was doing. It was daylight in America now, and Kathy was probably at school. Chantrea thought that Kathy must be wearing clean clothes, and that her hair must be beautiful and shining. As Chantrea tossed and turned, unable to get comfortable because her muscles hurt so much, Kathy was probably laughing at something, smiling in a way that looked just like Father, Kathy's Uncle Seth, did in the wedding picture.

She thought of the trip her family had planned to take to Ohio this summer. That would never happen now, would it? All she had was this one picture, but she reminded herself that there were many who had nothing at all.

But there were few chances to look at the picture. The soldiers seemed to watch them at all times.

Sometimes, Chantrea had to help one of her grandparents walk. Grandmother felt as light as a bird when she leaned against Chantrea. Beneath her *krama*, the red-and-white checkered scarf she wore around her head, her face grew darker and darker from the burning sun. Chantrea knew her own face looked the same.

One day, unable to stand any more cruelty, a man confronted the soldiers. He had been pushing his elderly father along the road in a hospital bed. To Chantrea, the old man looked like a bundle of sticks, his skin like a loose cloth laid over his bones. He had wailed like a child for the first few days, but was silent now.

"Please, sirs," the old man's son begged, his fingertips pressed together as he bowed with fearful respect, "my father is dying. If I could just take him into the shade, away from the sun, he could be at peace."

Chantrea watched as the soldier stared at the man with cold, hard eyes.

"You don't think *Angkar* knows what is best?" he demanded.

Angkar! Chantrea had grown to truly hate that word. The Khmer Rouge's special committee was hateful and cruel.

The man opened his mouth, but suddenly seemed

30

afraid to speak. Chantrea watched as a smile spread over the soldier's face, a smile that did not change the hardness of his eyes. He jumped from the truck, and, to Chantrea's surprise, came to help push the hospital bed off the road.

"Angkar will care for you," he said.

No one stopped. No one watched the soldier and the man wheel the bed from the road and into the nearby jungle. Chantrea glanced back over her shoulder, until Grandmother gave her a sharp tap and indicated she should watch the road ahead. A few moments later, two shots rang out from the trees. No one jumped, no one screamed. They had become used to the sounds of gunfire.

After that morning, only a few dared to ask for help. Some were taken into the woods and shot, some executed right where they stood. The people quickly learned that silence was best.

One day, soldiers came into the crowd and pointed to different people. When one of them tapped Chantrea on the shoulder, and then indicated each of her grandparents, Chantrea's heart sank. She knew they would be taken into the woods and shot. It did not matter that they'd committed no crime. For some reason, they displeased the Khmer Rouge soldiers and would die today.

Great relief washed over her as the group was separated from the larger crowd and led toward a rice field. Chantrea realized she wasn't going to be shot, after all. Instead, this group had been chosen to work on a rice farm. They passed workers who were already busy in the paddies. No one looked up at them. Chantrea thought she had never seen such frail, thin people.

Grandfather put an arm around her and whispered,

"Remember you are Mok Chantrea now, not Chantrea Conway. It is the only safe way."

"Yes, Grandfather," Chantrea whispered back. "I will remember."

The soldiers separated the men from the women. Grandmother, Chantrea, and five other women were given shelter in a little bamboo and thatch hut. Chantrea sat on a straw mat to rest, grateful to be off her sore feet. Her sandals had fallen apart days ago. Grandmother curled up on the mat next to hers and closed her eyes. The other women did the same. Some of them tried to catch a few precious moments of sleep. Chantrea recognized Chantou's mother, Sitha. The woman no longer mumbled about her dead daughter, but sat with a blank expression on her face.

Chantou's mother had lost a daughter, and Chantrea had lost her mother. She felt hot tears roll down her cheeks. How many more would die? Would Father rescue her in time? Where was he? How could he even find her?

Chantrea took the wedding picture out of her pocket and gazed at it for a long time.

"Chantrea!" Grandmother hissed.

She looked up to see a frightened look on Grandmother's face. The old woman wagged a finger at the snapshot.

"Put it away!" she ordered. "Do not let them see it!"

"Yes, Grandmother," Chantrea said, and slipped the picture back into her pocket.

No sooner did she do so than the door to the hut burst open. An armed soldier stood there with a grim-faced young woman. Chantrea thought she couldn't be much older than twenty, but her eyes were like hard pieces of ebony, as icy as the soldier's eyes. Chantrea wondered if she had a gun hidden in her *sampot*.

"On your feet!" the soldier barked, and waved his gun.

The women obeyed. They moved stiffly, like puppets.

"Today you will begin your training for a new life!" the soldier said. "Your past does not exist. What you did in your old life does not matter. You will follow Rann and she will teach you how to work as a noble farmer!"

Slowly, the women followed Rann out of the hut. Joined by others, they marched to a vast rice field. Rann showed them how to harvest the rice, and how to pull out weeds. The water actually felt good to Chantrea's aching feet. In the beginning, it was easy to pull the weeds. But as the day went on, her back seemed to scream out in pain. She glanced around herself and saw Grandmother in the distance. She hunched over, and moved as if every gesture hurt terribly. Poor Grandmother! Would she be able to survive this torture? And what was happening to Grandfather now?

At the peak of the day, they were given one hour to rest. But there was no sleep for the weary captives. They assembled in a large hut that had been lined with straw mats. The women and girls sat to one side, and the men and boys to the other. Chantrea looked for Grandfather, but could not see him. Each person was given a bowl of watery rice. Chantrea thought it was hardly enough food to keep a nightingale alive, let alone people who had worked hard for hours.

A man in an officer's uniform stepped up on the platform at the front of the room. Chantrea was so tired she hardly heard him as he spoke, but she didn't dare take her eyes from him. Soldiers watched the group, looking for any reason to lift their rifles.

"For years, our country has been slave to the whims of foreigners!" the officer shouted, so loud a flock of birds outside shot up to the safety of the sky. "But Angkar will change all that, and we will begin a new era of freedom! This is the Year Zero, the new beginning! Cambodia no longer exists. We now live in Democratic Kampuchea. Say it with me!"

"Democratic Kampuchea," the confused and tired group repeated.

"Louder!"

"Democratic Kampuchea!" they shouted.

Chantrea shouted with them, but in her mind she wondered why they had to change the country's name.

"All those who honored the regime of Lon Nol," the officer went on, "all those from the cities who brag about their fine educations and their money—you are the New People. We have no use for New People under Angkar! You must become as the Old People, as those noble peasants who worked the land and answered to no foreign master! You must give all your loyalty to Angkar, and Angkar will provide!"

On and on he yelled, until Chantrea thought she would collapse. What kind of crazy ideas did this man have? It seemed the Khmer Rouge blamed all of Cambodia's problems on the foreigners who had been in charge over the past centuries. The man spit out horrible curses against the Chinese and the French. He had no use for Americans, or the Vietnamese. Angkar, he explained, thought the best way to end years of grief would be to start

34

again. They truly were going to begin in Year Zero, as if Cambodia had no history at all. Everyone, without exception, would learn to work as a farmer. Those who disagreed would be punished.

At last he finished, and the assembly was allowed to break up and return to their huts. They had only a short time to rest before they were called out into the fields again. By the time Chantrea went to sleep that night, she could feel every muscle and joint in her body. But she did not complain about it. If Grandmother could keep silent, so could she.

In the darkness, Grandmother reached across the floor and took Chantrea's hand in her own. They held on to each other all through a night that was far too short. When Chantrea heard someone call out names, she did not open her eyes. Surely, this was all a dream. She would wake up in her safe, warm bed in Phnom Penh . . .

"Mok Chantrea!"

She did not move.

"Mok Chantrea!"

A sharp poke made her open her eyes. Grandmother knelt beside her with a look of fear on her face. Quickly, Chantrea jumped to her feet.

"Present!" she cried out.

How could she have been so foolish, she asked herself? She had ignored her Cambodian name!

Rann gave her a nasty look, then led the women out to the large hut for a breakfast of rice. When Chantrea came to the cauldron, she was waved away.

"No rice for you," the man at the pot said.

Slowly, Chantrea went to her seat. She had gone hungry a lot in the past days, and was certain she could go for a few more hours. No doubt this had happened because she hadn't answered to her name. As she sat, she noticed a young man looking at her from the men's group across the room. He was about seventeen or eighteen years old, and he gave Chantrea a little smile. His kind gesture made her feel a little better.

The same officer from yesterday made another speech, and asked those who had supported Lon Nol, Cambodia's former leader, to come forward. They would be forgiven, and all would be well again. One man slowly raised his hand. He shuffled forward and the officer hugged him tightly.

"What did you do in your old life?" the officer asked.

"I am Dr. Boua," said the man. He bowed forward. "If I could offer my services to Angkar, to help these people who need medical care, it would be an honor."

"And we would be honored to have you," the officer said. He looked at one of his men. "Go with Dr. Boua and ask of his ideas to help us."

There was a little smile on Dr. Boua's face as the soldier led him away. Chantrea saw that he trusted these men, but she would never trust them.

"Anyone else?"

A few more people came forward. One was a teacher and another an artist. They were also led away by soldiers. The officer seemed very pleased with them. No one else raised a hand. At last, breakfast was over. Chantrea was grateful to get away from the smells of rice she was not permitted to eat.

Today, Chantrea saw Grandfather lead a pair of oxen

across the nearby field. She wished she could wave to him, but didn't dare stop her work. She tried to keep her mind busy with happy thoughts of the past. She thought of playing baseball with Father and helping Mother cook. An American song popped into her head, and she tried to remember how nice it was to hear music, instead of the speeches about Angkar that played loudly through the speakers around the farm.

At last, the sun became too hot, and the people were allowed their afternoon break. They lined up for rice and water. But when it was Chantrea's turn, she was pulled off the line.

"Angkar wants to be certain you understand what is expected of you," said Rann. "What is your name, girl?"

"Mok Chantrea," Chantrea answered.

Rann slapped her across the face. Chantrea stumbled back, but managed not to fall. Tears spilled down her cheeks. Why was her answer wrong?

Now Rann asked for her name in the French language. Chantrea, despite her fear and pain, somehow remembered to pretend she did not understand. The woman asked her in English, too. Still, Chantrea shook her head as if she didn't understand. In the past days, she had seen several people punished for daring to speak a language other than Khmer.

At last, Rann seemed satisfied.

"You will have no rice today, Mok Chantrea," she said, and walked away. "I think you will not forget to answer to your name again."

Chantrea's face hurt so much she could not even look

up. She felt anger rising in her once again. How could a young girl act so cruelly?

She followed everyone to the rice fields. There, Grandmother whispered that she could rub some mud on herself to soothe her cheek. Chantrea did so, but it only helped the pain on her skin. The pain in her heart was much too deep. Why was this happening to her people? Why was there suddenly so much terror and hatred?

"Father, please come for me," she whispered as she yanked a weed out of the muddy water. "Please, please hurry!"

Chapter Four

CHANTREA was sound asleep on her mat, exhausted after a day in the heat without food, when she felt someone shake her. Instantly, she sat up and said, "Present!"

"Shh!" whispered a voice. "Follow me!"

Chantrea took a quick look at Grandmother's mat. The woman snored softly, sleeping deeply. Chantrea stood up and followed the shadowy figure out of the hut. Her heart pounded in terror. Surely one of the soldiers was about to punish her further for her mistake this morning.

But when she got outside, she saw that it was the young man who had smiled at her at breakfast.

"My name is Piarun," he said. "I know yours is Chantrea. Are you hungry?"

Chantrea nodded. Her heart still thumped, for she could not be certain if this was a trick.

"There are rabbits and lizards in the woods," Piarun said. "Some of us have found ways to sneak out of the camp and hunt them."

He began to hurry away. Chantrea, afraid to be left alone, followed him. The muddy ground felt warm beneath her bare feet. Once, just before they rounded the corner of a hut, Piarun held up a hand and stopped. He crept slowly forward, then indicated she could follow him. Chantrea felt a cold chill wash over her as she saw the guard who sat outside the hut, but soon realized he was asleep. She did not say a word to Piarun until they were deep in the woods.

"How long have you been here?" she asked.

"Six weeks," Piarun said. "They emptied out my city, Battambang."

"Battambang!" Chantrea cried. "My father was there. An American photographer. Did you see him?"

"I'm sorry, Chantrea," Piarun replied. "It's a big city, with many people, like Phnom Penh."

"You mean, like Phnom Penh used to be," Chantrea said, and thought of the ghost town she had left behind.

"You must be quiet, now," Piarun said. "We only have a short time."

Chantrea looked around, but could see little in the thick growth of trees.

"Are there others?"

"Yes, but you will never know of them," Piarun told her. "We must all be very careful."

Chantrea moved silently as she followed him. She watched as he peered at the ground. After a short time, he took off his shirt and leaped down at a low bush. When he came up again, something scrambled inside the cloth. He held it fast for only a moment, and the movement stopped. When he opened the shirt, Chantrea saw a dead lizard. To her surprise, Piarun tore it open with his fingers and started to clean it as if it were a fish. He handed a piece of its flesh to her. Chantrea's stomach reeled.

"I know it seems awful," Piarun said, "but you will learn to take food where you can get it. And you can't be sure they will feed you tomorrow."

Shaking, Chantrea took the cold meat into her hand.

"Best to swallow it quickly," Piarun suggested.

Chantrea put the meat into her mouth and swallow it without chewing. It left a strange taste on her tongue, but it wasn't as horrible as she'd thought. At least it was food. How long had it been since she last had meat? A month? A year? It could easily have been a thousand years, her old life seemed so far away.

They found and shared two more lizards, until Piarun said they had to go back or be caught. He took her to her hut. Grandmother was awake, but she said nothing to Chantrea. She simply took her hand and squeezed it, then went back to sleep.

The days and weeks passed with the same terrible routine. At every meal one of the officers made speeches about Angkar, and how wonderful it was. They were told their new leader, Pol Pot, would make Cambodia a great nation again. Only now they weren't allowed to call it Cambodia. It was Kampuchea under the Khmer Rouge. At mealtimes, more and more people came forward to confess their support of the old regime. Many of them began to agree with the speeches, and some even began to call each other comrade out in the fields.

They worked long, hot hours until the sun became so hot the guards themselves could not stand it. Everyone was given an hour to rest, and most tried to find a few minutes for sleep. Chantrea could never sleep in the terrible heat. Her back, legs, and arms simply hurt too much.

She began to look forward to the nights. It wasn't much cooler, but at least she did not have to listen to insane speeches about Angkar and Pol Pot. And she did not have to look at bodies scattered about the fields. Sometimes, the soldiers did not bother to hide the people they murdered. Rann told her group it was Angkar's way to help them remember who was in charge now, and what would happen if they disobeyed. Chantrea thought the ones with bags tied over their heads were the worst. She knew they had not died quickly. She prayed that would never happen to her.

Piarun came back for her many times over the next months. He was able to tell her about her grandfather. Chantrea was grateful to hear that Grandfather was doing as well as he could. Piarun said everyone liked Mok Meng, who had even made them laugh once or twice with his magic tricks.

"He pulled a small flat stone out of someone's ear," Piarun said one night.

"He used to use a *sen* for that," Chantrea said.

"I don't remember the last time I saw a *sen*," Piarun sighed. "Angkar says they are worthless now."

They walked deeper into the woods. Piarun reached

behind a tree and pulled out a spear he had made from a fallen branch. He had hidden it there a few nights earlier.

"Angkar! I hate that word," Chantrea growled. "I wish I would never hear it again."

"Many agree with you," Piarun said. "Chantrea, have you noticed something at the meals?"

"My parents would never have called that dirty watered-down rice gruel a meal," Chantrea grumbled.

Piarun stopped. He lifted the spear and flung it forward. When he pulled it up, there was a small rabbit on the end. Chantrea did not even flinch as she watched him pull it apart. She ate the raw meat without a word.

"Think of the people who have confessed to allegiance to Lon Nol," Piarun said. "Have you ever seen any of them again?"

Chantrea thought, and realized she hadn't.

"They are taking them away and killing them," Piarun said. "Anyone who is intelligent, who asks questions. Anyone who might try to fight them."

"Oh, no," Chantrea whispered. "My grandfather was a teacher!"

"Then he must never reveal that to the Khmer Rouge soldiers," Piarun said.

They ate in silence for a few more minutes.

"Something else, too," Piarun said. He spoke so suddenly in the darkness that Chantrea gasped. "Did you notice there are no little children here?"

Chantrea realized that it was true. She had just been too busy in the rice paddies to think about it.

"They take them away from their parents," Piarun said, "and put them into special schools to educate them in the ways of Angkar. They poison their minds and turn them into monsters."

He sighed and continued to eat in silence. Around them, the night was full of jungle noises.

"Are you finished?" he asked after a while. "We need to go back."

Chantrea had grown to love her nocturnal escapes with Piarun so much that she always hated to return to her hut.

"I wish we could stay out here and talk all night," she said.

"So do I," Piarun said.

She looked at him. Piarun's face seemed to glow in the moonlight that weaved its way through the thick canopy of leaves overhead.

"Why are you so nice to me?"

Piarun bowed his head. "I had a little sister, just about your age. The Khmer Rouge killed her, and my parents as well. You make me think of her."

"They killed my mother, too," Chantrea said.

Now Piarun looked up. "Chantrea, this can't last forever. Someone will stop these madmen!"

Chantrea thought of her father. When she first came to this terrible place, she had held onto the hope he would rescue her. Now she wasn't so certain. The Khmer Rouge were very powerful. Perhaps it was hard for Father to get to her. Still, she had to believe that Piarun was right, that this nightmare couldn't last forever.

She saved some of the rabbit meat and shared it with the others in her hut when she returned. Because she risked her own life to feed the other women, Chantrea had become like a hero to them. Sitha always gave her a big hug. Sometimes, the way Sitha clung to her, Chantrea thought she must be thinking of her dead daughter.

All the women vowed to protect her. But what could a small group of hungry, weak women do against strong soldiers with guns? Chantrea knew that something had to be done, but how? How could they ever escape?

Then one day, something happened that terrified her so much she knew she either had to get away, or die.

People constantly came and went from the camp. Chantrea knew that many who left weren't going to other farms, as promised, but to their deaths. But she had to believe that some really did make it to other places, because new people came to work at this farm every week.

She recognized many faces from Phnom Penh. At first, she had been terrified they would reveal her secret, or that they would tell the Khmer Rouge soldiers that Grandfather was once a teacher. But that didn't happen, and slowly she began to believe those who knew her family would remain true friends. But at the morning meal one day, she heard a familiar name that made her look up with a start.

"Funan Sothea!"

Yes, it was her classmate, the girl who had ridiculed her American name when they still lived in Phnom Penh. Sothea looked very different. Her moon-shaped face was gone after months of hunger, replaced by a skull-like mask of skin stretched over bone. But there was a hard glint in her eyes that made Chantrea feel icy inside. Rann had that same hard, hateful gaze. Chantrea also noticed that Sothea's nose was red and she sniffled with a cold.

"Despite sickness," the officer said to the group, "Funan Sothea has worked all this week in the fields without a minute of complaint!"

All week? Chantrea wondered. Why hadn't she seen her before?

"This is how we must all dedicate ourselves to Angkar! You must look at this fine young woman as an example!"

Sothea smiled a little, then sneezed. Everyone applauded her. She was allowed to leave the platform. As she passed Chantrea, she looked straight at her with the coldest, most evil smile Chantrea had ever seen. Chantrea's mouth went dry and she could hardly swallow the small amount of rice she had been given. Would Sothea tell the Khmer Rouge the truth?

––––––––––

DAYS passed. Chantrea hunted at night twice with Piarun. One night, they found three frogs and a rabbit, but on the other night there was only a lizard. She told Piarun about Sothea.

"The Khmer Rouge find enemies everywhere," Piarun said. "They don't need your old friend to turn them against you. You must live each day, Chantrea, and not worry about things you can't change."

Chantrea did worry, and a week later her worst nightmare came true. Instead of his usual speech, the officer barked out a list of names. Chantrea, Grandmother, Grandfather, and a few others were included. They marched forward, heads bowed. In all her months here,

Chantrea had never been this close to Grandfather. She was shocked by how old and haggard he looked. He was only fifty-six years old, but now he looked like a man who was nearly seventy. She wished she could hug him, but only dared to stare down at her own dirty, scabby feet.

"Angkar has always given you opportunity to confess your crimes," the officer said, "and has always had the heart to forgive the contrite."

Liar! Chantrea screamed in her mind. *You never forgive! You murder!*

"But here stands a group of dissidents who think they can fool Angkar with their lies! It has been brought to our knowledge that there is an American here!"

Chantrea stumbled a little. She felt a hand reach out to steady her. She dared look sideways to see that Grandfather held her by the elbow.

"Mok Chantrea is truly Chantrea Conway!" the officer cried out. "Her father is an American pig!"

Cries against Americans, and against Chantrea herself, filled the air. Chantrea looked up. Some of the women from her hut, women she'd helped to feed, screamed in anger at her. She searched the men's group for Piarun, but could not see him.

"Mok Meng is a teacher, one of the New People!" the officer screamed over the din of the crowd. The officer held up both arms and everyone fell instantly silent. They were as obedient as beaten dogs.

"You had your chance to confess but did not take it," he said. "It was the honesty of another in our group who brought the truth to me."

Weeks of starvation and hard work had dried all of

Chantrea's tears. She felt cold all over, as if she walked in a nightmare. This was not happening! She wasn't the one being escorted at gunpoint out of the tent. She was only thirteen. Someone else would die, not her!

"Heng Piarun!"

Chantrea gasped at the sound of that name. She looked up as Piarun was dragged forward.

"You have been accused of stealing food," the officer said.

Piarun said nothing as he was pushed toward Chantrea's group. Chantrea was certain he'd never stolen any food. Someone had seen him go out in the night to hunt. Was it Sothea? Chantrea thought it must be. For some reason, Sothea was filled with a hatred that made her turn in those she had known. When Duong Sothea was dragged forward a moment later, Chantrea knew she was right. Only Sothea could know that Sitha had been a friend of the Mok family. A few others were also brought out, and each one of them had been Chantrea's neighbors.

A soldier yanked Chantrea's arms behind her back. He moved roughly, making the rope cut into her wrists as he tied them. Other guards secured the remaining accused. The crowd of emaciated, sick and tired people around them shouted madly for their executions. The officer held up both his hands.

"Before they are taken to the deaths they deserve," he said, "these spies will first be taken away for questioning. We must be certain that all who work against Angkar are found!"

Spies? Chantrea wasn't sure she'd heard the word

correctly. Why did he think they were spies? They hardly had the energy to walk!

Grandfather began to plead for Grandmother's release.

"She is not an intellectual," he insisted. "She does not even know how to read! Please, she will be true to Angkar. Let her go!"

"Shut up, old man!" a soldier, a boy hardly older than Chantrea, snapped.

"I will never be true to evil, Meng," Grandmother said, as she glared defiantly at the boy soldier.

They were marched outside, past the people working in the fields, and forced onto the back of a truck. Chantrea found herself between Piarun and a man who had once sold fish in the market near her home. Her grandparents sat across from her. A guard sat at the back, his rifle resting across his lap. The driver, whom Chantrea could see through a little window, kept his own rifle propped on the seat next to him. The truck began to roll down the rough, bumpy road. Chantrea wondered where they were going, and then decided she didn't want to know. Whatever their destination, it would be horrible.

The only sound now was Sitha's soft whimpering. Sitha had buried her face in a blue and white checkered *krama*. Chantrea was more certain than ever that Sothea had done this, for who else would turn in Chantou's mother, a woman who had done nothing wrong? She wondered what rewards Sothea would receive for her betrayal.

They drove for a long time. The guard at the back of the truck fell asleep. When she heard him snoring, Chantra dared to speak to Piarun.

"Why do they think we are spies, Piarun?" she asked in a whisper.

"These people are suspicious of everyone, Chantra," Piarun answered.

"I'm so sorry I got you into trouble, Piarun," Chantrea said. She thought her tears might come at last.

"It isn't your fault," Piarun insisted. "I probably would have been caught sooner or later."

They were silent for a while. Then Chantrea spoke again.

"They are going to ask us questions," she said. "I wonder what that means."

"You know what it means, Chantrea," Piarun said in a grim voice.

Yes, she knew. Even at thirteen she knew that, to the Khmer Rouge, questioning was just another word for torture.

"But . . ."

"Shh!" Grandmother hissed. She looked at the sleeping guard, then back at Chantrea. Immediately, Chantrea fell silent. She put her head on Piarun's shoulder and closed her eyes. Fear and sickness exhausted her, and she soon fell asleep.

Something that moved against her hands awakened her a while later. It took her a moment to realize it was Piarun's own hands, as he worked at her ties! Somehow, he had managed to free himself. She glanced sideways at the guard and saw he was still asleep. No doubt he didn't feel he needed to stay awake to watch these weak and terrified prisoners. Chantrea looked at Piarun, who gave her a little nod. As soon as she was free, she began to work on the fish seller's ropes. He looked at her with surprise, but said nothing.

Slowly, steadily, one person helped untie another. The driver kept his eyes on the road and saw nothing. The guard at the back snored in a deep sleep. Sitha seemed ready to cry out loud now. Her face was a mask of sheer terror. But Grandfather rested a gentle hand over her mouth and silenced her.

Piarun took off his ragged shirt and crawled toward the sleeping guard. Just a second before he reached him, the truck hit a pothole and jolted the man awake. A look of complete surprise came over his face, but Piarun jumped at him and covered his head with the shirt. They scrambled together, and somehow the guard was able to feel for the trigger of his rifle. A shot rang out, and someone screamed as one of the prisoners fell to the floor.

The truck's brakes squealed as the driver slammed to a stop. He came around to the back of the truck, rifle in hand. But Grandfather produced a small, pointed stick from his sleeve and jammed it into the guard before he could even aim his gun. Chantrea had seen him make many things appear from his shirt, but never a weapon!

There was no time to think how clever he was, to use his magic for their escape. He grabbed Chantrea with one hand and Grandmother with another. They ran like frightened rabbits into the nearby jungle. They did not stop or even look back. Chantrea could hear gunshots ringing out from the road. She saw that a few others had managed to get away, but where was Piarun?

"Keep running!" Grandfather ordered.

Somehow, Chantrea's weak legs and emaciated body

managed to move her deeper and deeper into the jungle. At last, Grandmother begged to stop. There was a huge tree nearby, a 100-foot banyan with shoots that reached out from the main tree to make new trunks. It offered a perfect hiding place, where Chantrea and her grandparents could watch and wait. All was silent. They were alone in the dark, thick jungle. But how long would it be before the soldiers came back with a patrol to hunt them down?

Chapter Five

CHANTREA watched a viper slither just a few inches in front of her nose. She held her breath so she wouldn't cry out, even though one bite from the poisonous snake might kill her. She looked past the thick, trunklike shoots of the banyan tree, to where her grandparents were crouched down in their own hiding place. Grandmother's eyes were closed, her head turned into Grandfather's shoulder. Grandfather's eyes widened in alarm when he saw the viper. He gave his head a shake that warned Chantrea to remain frozen.

But the snake didn't really frighten Chantrea. She would rather die from a snake bite than be killed by the Khmer Rouge soldiers. The two guards had gone back for help, and Chantrea could hear the shouts of the patrol that searched for them.

Just a few minutes after the snake had disappeared

into the jungle, Chantrea saw a pair of army boots appear just beyond her hiding place. She hugged herself tightly and watched them with wide eyes. If the soldier up there looked down into the thick tangle of roots, he would see the light-colored rag of her T-shirt.

Rain had formed a small creek at the base of the tree, and the murky water was up to Chantrea's waist. Her torn jeans did little to protect her, and she felt something long and slimy brush by her thin legs. Her heart began to pound and her stomach twisted. She was terrified that if the creature bit her, she would scream and alert the soldier. To her relief, the unseen animal went on its way just as the snake had done. Perhaps it only saw her as another root of the tree.

The soldier turned a little, and Chantrea gasped in horror. A blue-and-white checkered *krama* hung from one of his belt loops. Sitha had been the only one on the truck who wore a scarf of that color. There was a patch of blood on it as big as a mango. Chantrea knew that Sitha must be dead.

She began to shake all over. Had the soldier heard her gasp? Would he reach down and drag her out? Would he beat her until she was forced to say where her grandparents had gone? She knew she could not stand very much torture. She was weak and frail after months of hard work and little food.

But the soldier turned and walked away. Perhaps it was a miracle, or perhaps all the noises of the jungle had masked the sound she had made.

The patrol searched for hours, even through the hottest part of the day. Chantrea was grateful the big old tree provided some protection from the steady rain. But the water was hot and mucky and gnats and mosquitoes feasted on her. She had several fresh cuts from the run into the jungle that attracted the stinging insects. But she did not dare slap at them. She was afraid that the soldiers would hear the sounds.

There was no way to tell how long she huddled there. She looked up through the weave of the roots at the pale gray sky. The rain had stopped. For a time, she could see the sun, then it disappeared from her view. The day began to grow dark, and she grew weary. She realized the soldiers' shouts had faded away.

As the sun set and the day cooled, she began to fall asleep. She almost screamed out loud when she felt someone grab her by the wrist.

"It's Grandfather!" she heard him say.

She let him pull her up. Grandmother stood beside him, her hair tangled with leaves. Her soaked dress hung limply on her thin frame.

"You must have fallen asleep, Chantrea," Grandfather said. "You were about to slip under the water."

Chantrea looked around. It was almost completely dark now, the crescent moon offering only meager light.

"Are the soldiers gone?" she asked in a small voice.

"Yes, I think so," Grandfather said. "But they will be back at light. We must be as far away as possible by then. We'll have to walk in the darkness."

Chantrea looked around, but she couldn't see much through the thick trees.

"Where is everyone else?" she asked. "Did they escape, too? Where is Piarun?"

"Piarun has saved us," Grandfather said in a sad voice. "We must make our way to freedom now."

"With Piarun?" Chantrea asked, hopefully.

But Grandfather shook his head. Chantrea thought of the gunshots she'd heard when they first ran into the jungle. She understood that the soldiers had killed Piarun, a boy who had become like a brother to her. She felt grief and fury all mixed up inside, but she couldn't cry. It was as if her eyes were too weary from the sight of so much killing that they could not make tears.

"I will never forget my friend, Grandfather," she said softly.

Grandfather nodded and put an arm around her shoulders.

"Meng, if we are to go, let's go at once," Grandmother said. "We must not waste time."

"You are right, Teva," Grandfather said. "Follow me, but move quietly. We can't be sure that all the soldiers are gone."

Chantrea's heart leaped. "Grandfather, are they hiding out, waiting for us?"

"I don't know, Chantrea," Grandfather said. "All I know is that we must get as far away as we can. To stay will mean to die."

So they began to make their way through the hot, thick, dark jungle. Chantrea's heart beat so loudly that she was certain it would alert any soldier hidden nearby. Once, she heard a low growling. She hunched up her shoulders as she walked, and waited for a tiger to spring at her. But no animal leaped from the shadows.

They walked for hours. Sometimes they moved

quickly through the more open sections, sometimes they moved slowly over thick roots and low-growing plants. They remained as silent as possible, even when they saw the skeletons of murdered people in one clearing. But deep into the night, Chantrea thought of a question.

"Grandfather, where are we going?"

"Northwest," Grandfather replied. "That will take us to Thailand. I have heard rumors that there are people there who will help us."

"But only rumors," Grandmother warned.

"What if they make us go back?" Chantrea asked in a frightened voice.

"Hush, Teva," Grandfather commanded. "Do not frighten the girl. Take it easy, Chantrea, it will be all right."

In the darkness, Chantrea could not help a little smile to hear her grandfather say "take it easy." She hadn't heard him use an American expression in months and it made her feel a little better. For just a moment, it was almost the way it had been before the Khmer Rouge took over. How she wished Grandfather could truly show his sense of humor again! But how could they be happy, when they were weak, hungry, and frightened?

At last, Grandfather stopped. The sky was growing lighter. Chantrea's feet burned and her legs felt as if her knees had turned to rocks. They had walked all night.

"It's almost dawn," Grandfather said. "Here is a low cave where we can sleep for the day. I think we will be safe here."

"How far did we come, Grandfather?" Chantrea asked.

"I don't really know," Grandfather admitted. "But I think only a few miles. I'm afraid we must be ready to walk for many weeks to safety."

"I don't care how long it takes us," Grandmother said. "I will not be taken prisoner again."

Grandfather crouched down now and looked into the mouth of the cave, darker than the dark woods that surrounded it.

"What if something lives in there?" Grandmother asked.

Grandfather took a long stick and poked it into the cave. Chantrea heard it strike the walls at the sides. Nothing came out to attack them, and Grandfather decided it was empty.

"Help me cover the entrance," he said.

Chantrea and her grandparents pulled old branches and vines from the jungle floor and scattered them over and around the cave. The sky above them grew rosy with the first light of dawn.

"Good," Grandfather said. "No one will see us in here. We can sleep safely until it is dark again."

Chantrea didn't believe she would ever be able to sleep again, but as soon as she lay down inside the dark, cool cave, she drifted off. She slept deeply, and sometime in the night she had a dream. In the dream, she was in the rice field as Rann screamed at her. Sothea called her terrible names: ugly American, American spy, traitor pig. Then, suddenly, a huge dragon appeared in the sky. Father straddled its long, scaly neck. He had come to rescue her at last!

The dragon spit out fire and burned away all the rice

fields and the people who followed Angkar. Somehow, though, its flames did not touch the prisoners. The beast landed on the ashes, and her father jumped down. He ran to Chantrea with his arms outstretched.

"Chantrea! Chantrea!"

"Chantrea, wake up!"

Grandmother's voice broke through the dream. Chantrea opened her eyes to see it had grown dark again.

"I'm hungry," she whispered. Her voice was hoarse. "And thirsty."

"Grandfather has found us some papaya to eat," Grandmother said.

Chantrea followed her out of the cave. They sat on the ground and shared fruit. Chantrea was certain she had never tasted anything as delicious in her life. The juicy pulp helped soothe her throat and took a little of the sting out of her stomach. They ate quickly and soon were on their way again.

For the next three weeks, they followed the same routine: They hid in the daylight and moved at night. They found fruit to eat in the jungle, and rubbed mud on themselves to soothe the bites of insects. They cringed and held each other whenever a plane passed overhead, afraid a bomb would be dropped. Sometimes, when the moonlight shone through the trees, Chantrea took out the wedding picture. It was wrinkled and worn, but it still brought her much comfort.

Chantrea could sometimes see a road through the trees, but Grandfather explained that they did not dare walk on it.

"If there are patrols," he said, "they would stay on that road."

One early morning, they came across the body of a man. The leaves and twigs on the jungle floor around him were spattered with blood.

"He must have stepped on a land mine," Grandfather said quietly. "I've heard there are thousands of them hidden in these jungles."

That night, Chantrea's dreams were haunted by a ghost with no legs. The next day, she walked more carefully than ever, terrified she would hear that deadly click beneath her feet that meant she'd landed on one of the hidden mines.

By the fourth week, Chantrea was certain they would never reach the border.

"Grandfather, how do we know we are going the right way?" she asked.

"You know the sun sets in the east, don't you?" Grandfather said.

"Oh, yes," Chantrea replied. "And if we walk the opposite way, that is west. But, Grandfather, how do we know we are moving to the north?"

Now Grandfather stopped. Chantrea and Grandmother stopped, too.

"Listen hard, Chantrea," he said. "Do you hear the sound of water?"

It took a few moments to separate the noise from all the other sounds of the jungle, but Chantrea did hear it.

"Yes, Grandfather, I do," she said.

"That is the Tonle Sap River," Grandfather said. "I'm using it to guide us toward the northwest. We will follow it until we reach Tonle Sap Lake. Then we will follow the Sangker River west to the Thailand border."

At that moment, Chantrea thought that Grandfather was the most clever man in all the world. How could Angkar hate someone who was so clever? Why did they kill the educated people? But she already knew the answer to that: Smart people ask questions, and the Angkar did not want to answer them.

Another week went by. Sometimes, they heard the shouts of soldiers as they passed close to work farms. Once, very early in the morning, Chantrea had dared to peek through some thick bushes. She saw hundreds of workers digging ditches, as armed guards stood by.

Whenever she could, Chantrea used the hunting skills Piarun had taught her to catch frogs and lizards for meat. The jungle was a bounty of fruits and vegetables. Sometimes, when they ate, monkeys watched them from the trees above. Chantrea thought they were funny. But she didn't like to think of the bigger beasts that might also watch them, perhaps thinking of a tasty meal.

"Are there many tigers?" she asked Grandfather.

"I think I saw one about a week ago," Grandfather said. "But I wouldn't worry, Chantrea. There is so little meat on us that we would make a poor meal for even a tiger cub."

"It is not the tigers that worry me, Meng," Grandmother said.

Chantrea knew that Grandmother was still afraid they would be caught. There had been people nearby, but no one had come out to confront them. Perhaps some of them were also escaped prisoners, too frightened to reveal themselves. Sometimes, Chantrea would wake up in the night, in a cave or behind thick bushes. She would hear footsteps nearby, or voices, and she would not be able to sleep for a long time.

At last, they reached the Tonle Sap Lake. Many people worked nearby, harvesting rice or catching fish. They had passed other farms along the way, but this area was busier than any of the others. And there seemed to be many more soldiers with guns.

"We must be more careful than ever here," Grandfather whispered.

He had led them even deeper into the jungle, as far away from the soldiers as possible. Chantrea hardly slept that night. She dreamed of soldiers with insane smiles on their faces who shot everyone in sight. When Grandmother shook her awake in the night, she almost screamed.

"Hush!" Grandmother ordered. "We must go now!"

They followed Grandfather, and made a wide circle around the lake region. Chantrea was grateful when they left the lake behind. But Grandfather did not take them closer to the Sangker River for several days. He told Grandmother it wasn't safe yet.

One night, Chantrea heard the sound of a train as it rushed by. She thought of the people who might be onboard. Were they prisoners on the way to work farms, or were they leaving this awful place? Then she remembered the train passed through Battambang, the last place she knew her father had been.

"Grandfather," she said, "will we pass near Battambang? My father . . ."

"Chantrea, your father could no longer be there," Grandfather said gently. "If he did not evacuate months ago he . . ."

Grandfather stopped himself. Chantrea knew he meant to say, "He is dead." But she didn't believe that for a moment.

"You're right," she said in a quiet voice. "My father is not there now. He escaped and is safe."

The next night, they cut down to the banks of the river. Grandfather stopped to study a grove of bamboo trees. Chantrea tried to ask what he was doing, but Grandmother said, "Let him be." After a long while, Grandfather turned to them.

"Chantrea, look about the ground for loose vines," he said, "anything that we can use like rope. Teva, help me pick up the bamboo sticks that have fallen to the ground."

"What do you have in mind, Meng?" Grandmother asked.

"We must be very close to the border by now," Grandfather said. "I have not heard nor seen signs of a patrol for many days now. If we build a raft, perhaps we can float along the river."

"A raft!" Chantrea cried. "Oh, Grandfather, you're so clever!"

Grandfather smiled at her. He kept his mouth closed, as if to hide his teeth. Once, before Angkar, they had been white and straight. Now they were rotted by sickness and hunger. Chantrea ran her tongue along her own teeth. She had lost one just a few days ago. Grandmother had said it was only a baby tooth, but had looked concerned. Later,

Chantrea heard her whisper to Grandfather that the sooner they got proper nourishment, the better.

Together, they built the raft. Chantrea was amazed at Grandfather's skill. The raft was so sturdy that she was not the least bit afraid to get on it. But Grandmother hesitated.

"What of crocodiles, Meng?"

"They will leave us alone, as the tigers do," Grandfather insisted. "We have no choice, Teva. We must move forward."

So Grandmother let herself be pulled onto the little boat. Slowly, quietly, Grandfather guided it along the river with a long bamboo pole. Sometimes, Chantrea could see golden eyes stare at them from the thick jungle. When the sun began to rise, they had traveled quite a long way— much farther than they could have done on foot. Grandfather pulled the raft to the shore.

"We must take it apart now," he said.

"Oh, no, Grandfather," Chantrea protested. "All our work, and we have to destroy it?"

"Would you want us to leave it where a Khmer Rouge soldier might see it?" Grandmother asked.

Chantrea understood, and helped untie the vines. They hid the parts of the boat in the reeds and walked into the trees. Grandfather found a good place to hide, as he had done every dawn for the past weeks. Chantrea felt so safe with him that it was easy to fall asleep after a meal of breadfruit. When night came again, they built the raft once more.

As they floated along the river, Grandfather softly hummed a tune. It had been one that Chantrea's father really liked, an American rock and roll song. Chantrea's heart ached for her parents. The moon had waned to a sliver, and when she tried to look at the wedding picture, she could not see her parents' smiling faces.

Chantrea closed her eyes and said a little prayer to Buddha that one day soon she would find her father again. Then, just to be safe, she said a prayer to the god her father honored: Jesus. Maybe the two ancient ones could help her.

A little while later, she felt a tap on her shoulder. She opened her eyes to see the sky was pink with dawn's light.

"We'll pull ashore now," Grandfather said. "Be quiet and careful, Chantrea. I think that we must be very, very close to the border. There could be soldiers."

Grandfather steered the boat into the reeds that lined the river. Together, they took the boat apart and scattered the pieces of vine and bamboo. Then they went to look for the day's hiding place.

Suddenly, they heard someone shout. Footsteps pounded on the jungle floor, coming after them. Chantrea gasped and clung to her grandfather in terror. It could not be. They could not have come this far, only to be captured by Khmer Rouge soldiers this close to freedom!

Chapter Six

THEY rushed into the trees, but it was too late. Right behind them, someone yelled, "Halt!" in Khmer. The three fugitives stopped in a clearing. Chantrea heard the sounds of footsteps that crushed twigs and dead leaves on the jungle floor. She closed her eyes and waited for the click of a rifle that would kill them one by one, without questions.

"Turn around, please," a man's voice said.

Slowly, they obeyed. They had learned not to hesitate when the Khmer Rouge gave an order. But when she turned, Chantrea felt as if someone had reached down and taken two great stones from her shoulders. These were not Khmer Rouge soldiers at all. One of them had hair as light as sunshine, and the other was a man with black skin and a beard. They were both dressed in khaki shirts and pants, and the white man wore a wide-brimmed hat. They both carried rifles, which they now held pointed to the ground. They looked at each other, and then the black man said in English, "Civilians, Tommy," he said. "Looks like they've come a long way."

"We have," Grandfather said. "We have trekked through this jungle for many weeks."

Chantrea's stomach twisted to hear Grandfather speak English, a language she had not heard in months. Maybe these men had used it to trick them! She backed up a step, her heart sick. Now these men, who might be allies of the Khmer Rouge, would shoot them because Grandfather dared to use a foreign, forbidden tongue.

Then the yellow-haired man smiled at her. It was not the false smile of the soldiers who guarded the rice farm. Those men's smiles never touched their eyes, but this man's blue eyes were warm and kind. She hoped she did not have to be afraid.

"It's all right, little girl," the yellow-haired man said. "We're here to take you to safety."

"Then there is a place for us?" Grandmother asked. "It's not a rumor?"

"Many places," said the black man. He spoke Khmer as Grandmother did. "Although . . ."

Before he could finish, Grandmother burst into tears. She threw her arms around the black man and sobbed. He patted her bony back as her thin and sickly frame shook. Chantrea looked up at Grandfather with questioning eyes. She had never seen Grandmother cry like that, not even when Mother died. Chantrea was a little scared to see her so emotional.

"She is happy we are safe now," Grandfather explained.

Chantrea felt her heart skip a beat. Safe . . . what a wonderful word. From the time the Khmer Rouge soldiers had emptied her city, she had never thought she'd feel safe again.

"We won't be safe until we're over the border, sir," said the yellow-haired man. "Come with us. We're going to the Kamput refugee camp."

They followed the two men to a road, where they were surprised to see a truck filled with other refugees. There were young and old people and a few children. One woman cradled a baby in her arms. Its weak little body was wrapped in a dirty, ragged blanket. Chantrea looked at all of them, but there were no familiar faces. She wondered how many others had run away from the Khmer Rouge. Had some of them been in the woods nearby as they traveled? On those nights she'd heard voices and footsteps, had that been other fugitives instead of soldiers?

The yellow-haired man, who sat at the back of the truck, told him that his name was Tommy Fordham. The black man, who climbed in next to the driver, was Jack VanBuren. They explained that they were volunteers who sometimes crossed the border in search of refugees. As Chantrea began to feel more comfortable, she noticed how clean they were. And how well fed! She looked around at the other refugees on the back of the truck and realized how terrible she must appear herself. Her hair was matted and filthy with bits of wood and leaves. Her skin was painted brown with dried mud and red with the blood of dozens of mosquito bites she'd scratched. She looked down at her hands and saw fingers that looked like sticks. Her knees poked through her torn jeans like two doorknobs, and her feet looked as if someone had stretched tan leather over small bundles of twigs.

But, she thought to herself, *I am safe now. We are all safe. And it won't be long before Father comes for us.*

"How is it you speak English so well?" Tommy asked Grandfather.

Even though he was weak and tired, Grandfather pulled himself up as tall as he could and looked into the younger man's blue eyes.

"I'm a schoolteacher," he said. "I taught English at a high school in Phnom Penh. And I sometimes helped foreigners translate Khmer."

How proud he sounded, Chantrea thought. And how wonderful that he could boast of his work. He did not have to hide it as he had been forced to do by the Khmer Rouge.

"Well, that ought to be a big help to you," Tommy said. "If you want to go to America, you're more likely to get passage if you speak English."

"America?" Chantrea echoed. "Will we go to America, Grandfather?"

She remembered now that Father had planned to take her and Mother there this summer, before the Khmer Rouge had destroyed their lives. She had been excited about the trip, but now she was nervous. It would have been all right to visit, but she didn't want to make it her new home!

"I don't know, Chantrea," Grandfather said. "I have to consider what is best for us; for you, especially."

"A lot of people want to go," Tommy said. "But it's

hard to get there. You need a sponsor, and there aren't enough sponsors willing to take refugees. It is not only Cambodians who want to go, but Laotians and Vietnamese, too."

Chantrea thought about all those people running away from grief. And they wanted to go to America. She thought about her grandparents, her uncle, and her cousins who lived in Ohio. She had enjoyed her visit there a few years ago, but had been glad to come back home to Cambodia. Now it seemed Grandfather may decide to go there. But how long would they stay? Would they live there?

"Do you know Ohio, America?" she asked.

Tommy laughed. "How do you know about Ohio, little girl?"

"My name is Chantrea Conway," Chantrea said. It sounded so good to be able to say her American name at last. "My father is from Ohio. His name is Seth Conway. He takes pictures for an American magazine. It's called *American World View.*"

Now Tommy's eyes widened, and a big smile spread across his face.

"Well, it sounds to me like you'll be one of the lucky ones," he said. "We'll just find your daddy, and he'll come for you, before you know it."

Chantrea smiled up at Grandfather.

"Did you hear? Did you hear, Grandfather?" she asked. "They are going to find Father for us!"

"It is wonderful news," Grandfather said with a smile.

Chantrea turned to tell Grandmother, but the old woman was fast asleep.

71

"Poor Teva," Grandfather said. "She is so tired."

"She'll be able to rest safely once we reach the camp," Tommy said. "All of you will be able to rest."

"And eat?" a young woman asked.

Tommy nodded. "There is rice for everyone. But, unfortunately, our supplies are running low. You won't be able to feast, but you won't go hungry."

Grandfather put an arm around Chantrea's shoulders. She leaned against him, closed her eyes, and let the steady rhythm of the truck's engine lull her to sleep.

Safe at last, she thought, safe at last.

A short time later, she felt a tap on her shoulder and woke up. Grandfather pointed, and she saw the two tall guard towers that jutted over the tops of the trees. The truck pulled into a lot surrounded by a barbed-wire fence.

It looks just like a prison, Chantrea thought, and moved closer to Grandfather.

Tommy tried to reassure everyone.

"The guards are there to watch for any enemy who might try to cross into Thailand," he said. "They won't hurt you."

Most of the passengers still looked wary. Maybe the American man was right. There was a lot of fighting at the borders. But maybe those guards were also there so no one could leave, and move farther into Thailand.

Tommy and Jack helped the passengers out of the truck. The weak and tired refugees moved like snails.

"Look!" a young man cried. "It's like a city!"

Chantrea stood up and gazed out over a sea of blue and brown. There were so many thatch-roofed bamboo huts and tents made of blue plastic, all lined in neat rows, that she couldn't even begin to count them. Even though she knew many cities had been emptied, as Phnom Penh had been, she never imagined so many thousands of people could be in one small place.

"How many people are here?" she asked as she moved to the back of the truck.

"There are at least a thousand people here," Tommy said. "And more come every day. This is a very small camp compared to some of the others along the border."

Chantrea felt numb as Jack helped her off the back of the truck. A thousand refugees, and more in other camps. So many lost, homeless people. And now there were twelve more. Grandfather held both Grandmother's and Chantrea's hands. Frightened and confused, everyone stood still. What were they to do now?

For the past months, Chantrea's days had been filled with rules. She was told when to eat, when to sleep. No one in the camps had dared make a move without permission. Now, it seemed they had all forgotten what freedom was about.

"Let's get you guys settled in someplace," Jack said.

Tommy took half the newcomers, while Chantrea and the others followed Jack. He led them to a large tent, where the floor had been lined with straw mats. Chantrea thought of the small tent she had shared with the other women at the rice farm. But it only took her a moment to realize there was something very, very different about this place.

She actually heard people laughing!

She looked at her grandparents. They also stared in wonder at the little clusters of people scattered throughout the tent. Grandmother blinked and rubbed her eyes as if she were in a dream. People did not move like living statues here, afraid of every noise they heard.

"Nary!" Jack called.

A teenaged girl who sat on one of the mats nearby turned to look up at him. When she stood, she moved so gracefully that Chantrea was reminded of the Court Dancers she had once seen. Her black hair hung down to her waist. Her skin was as smooth as ivory, and her eyes were surrounded by thick black lashes. She smiled, and Chantrea thought she was almost as beautiful as Mother had been.

"Nary, honey," Jack said, "would you find the Mok family a place in here?"

Jack looked at Grandfather. "Nary is our ambassador. She knows everything there is to know about the camp. If you have any questions, you can ask her."

"But you are so young," Grandfather said.

Nary bowed a little. "I am the oldest in my family now. My parents, grandparents, and older brothers were all killed by the Khmer Rouge. I ran away with my baby sisters."

"The Khmer Rouge killed my daughter, Chantrea's mother," Grandfather told her.

Nary looked at Chantrea.

"What of your father, little sister?"

Chantrea liked the way this beautiful girl called her "little sister." It made her feel welcome, like family.

"My father is an American," Chantrea said. "He will be coming for me, soon."

Now a sad look passed over Nary's beautiful face. But

it vanished quickly, and she smiled again. Chantrea had seen that same look on Grandmother's face. She could tell that Nary didn't believe Father would ever come.

"Let's not talk now," Nary said. "Follow me and I'll show you a place where you can sleep tonight."

She lead them to a space on the far side of the tent. Now Chantrea noticed that other families had brought things with them. There were cooking pots and blankets and even little toys. A small boy, who seemed no older than two, crawled over to Chantrea as he pushed a little wooden cart.

"Yem, come back here," his mother called.

The baby giggled but did not move. His mother came to get him. She nodded briefly at the Mok family, then returned to her mat with Yem in her arms.

"I'll see to it that you have blankets tonight," Nary said. "Meanwhile, perhaps you would like to wash yourselves? There is water for bathing in the blue tent next door."

Nary explained that the men and women took turns. When Chantrea and Grandmother entered, they recognized two women from the truck. The water felt wonderful to Chantrea, as it washed away weeks of mud and soothed her bug bites and the itchy scabs on her arms and legs. It was cold, but it might easily have been the warm, fragrant water of a spa. Grandmother helped her wash the dirt from her hair, then Chantrea did the same for her grandmother. They were still dressed in rags when they finished, but at least Chantrea could see her own skin again.

After the women finished, the men took their turn. Grandfather came out after only a few minutes. With his hair combed and his face washed, he almost looked like the handsome man he'd been before Phnom Penh was captured, Chantrea thought.

"I smell rice," Chantrea said.

"There seem to be pots everywhere," Grandfather replied.

Nary came up to them.

"You'll share dinner with my family," she offered.

Soon, they were gathered in a circle around a cooking fire. Nary introduced her sisters, four-year-old twins named Dara and Kalliyan. Chantrea liked to hear those names again. Whatever had become of her friend Kalliyan? she wondered.

But she did not think about her lost friend for long. Nary ladled a heaping plateful of wild rice into a wooden bowl and handed it to Grandfather. Grandmother's bowl came next. When it was finally Chantrea's turn, she almost passed out at the wonderful smell. This was not the dirty, watery rice gruel she had been forced to eat at the camp. This rice was fluffy and fragrant, a meal fit for Buddha.

Suddenly, Chantrea's eyes filled with tears. She hadn't cried for weeks, but now she could not stop herself.

"My granddaughter is touched by your kindness," said Grandfather.

Nary put a hand over Chantrea's. "It's all right. I only wish there was more to offer. Jack says we are waiting for supplies to come in. Other countries are helping us as best as they can."

Chantrea blinked away her tears.

"America, too?"

"Yes, America, too," Nary said.

"Chantrea, eat your rice before it grows cold," Grandmother ordered.

Chantrea began to shovel large spoonfuls of the wonderful rice into her mouth. All those months on the farm, she had been given so little time to eat that she had learned to finish her meals as quickly as possible.

"Slow down, little sister," Nary urged. "No one will take your food away, and no one will rush you. It is different here."

But Chantrea realized she had already cleaned out her bowl. She bowed her head and felt ashamed for eating like a pig in front of this kind, beautiful girl.

Nary didn't say a word. She simply spooned more rice into Chantrea's dish. This time, Chantrea ate slowly.

That night, for the first time in months, Chantrea went to bed with a full stomach and a clean body. She had been rescued from her country's tormentors, and she was safe. Could it be very long before she'd see her father?

Chapter Seven

NARY brought clothes for Chantrea and her grand-parents. Chantrea received a sleeveless dress, some underwear, and a pair of sandals. The dress was faded and the sandals worn, but she didn't care. They were clean and neat, and that was all that mattered. It felt wonderful to put on something new after wearing the same ragged clothes for many months.

Although they felt safer now, Chantrea and her grandparents were still very weak from their long trek out of Cambodia. They rested in their tent for the next two weeks. At first, it was hard to sleep with all the noise. The sound of planes that flew overhead was the worst, because the Moks were worried about bombs. But soon, they even grew used to that.

"Nary, what do you do here?" Chantrea asked one day.

"I work in one of the hospital tents," Nary said.

"You're a nurse?" Chantrea asked. "I thought maybe you were a dancer. You're so very graceful."

Nary laughed. "Yes, I was a dancer, before the Khmer Rouge. I danced with the Classical Dance Company of Cambodia. But they closed down my company and burned our theater to the ground."

"I'm sorry," Chantrea said.

"I will dance again someday," Nary insisted. "Meanwhile, there are so many sick and hurt people here that the doctors and nurses don't have enough help."

"I can help," Chantrea offered.

Nary smiled at her. "You need to get your strength back, little sister. You've suffered too long."

"I feel fine," Chantrea insisted, although it was a lie. She still ached all over. "I have rested two weeks, and now I want to do something."

"You'll be even better in a few more weeks," Nary said. "And then I'll ask the doctors what help you can give them."

She reached out and stroked Chantrea's cheek.

"I have to go," Nary said. "I'll be back at lunchtime."

Nary moved from the tent like a light-footed fawn. Chantrea looked down at her own scabby, skinny body and suddenly felt very ugly and awkward.

"Father wouldn't think I was ugly," she said out loud.

"Ug-lee?" little Yem echoed, and looked up at her.

The toddler played with a ball someone had made from strips of rags. Chantrea patted him on the head, then left the tent. She couldn't see Grandmother anywhere, but found Grandfather with a group of men. Respectfully, she

80

stood a short distance away and waited until Grandfather saw her. He smiled and held out an arm. She hurried into his embrace.

"Do you feel better this morning?" he asked.

"Yes, Grandfather," Chantrea replied. "I wanted to help Nary in the hospital tent, but she says I need to get my strength back."

"She is right," Grandfather said. "It is a good idea to take it easy."

This time, Chantrea did not smile to hear Grandfather speak like an American.

"What's wrong, Chantrea?" he asked.

Chantrea didn't want to speak her private thoughts in front of the other men. She bowed her head. Grandfather led her away, to a spot where they could talk. They couldn't really be alone, not in a camp full of people, but at least the space between two tents offered a little privacy.

"Tell me what's wrong, Chantrea," Grandfather said. "Are you afraid we'll have to go back?"

"No, Grandfather," Chantrea said. She looked up at him, and saw love in his dark eyes. "Grandfather, will I ever see my father again?"

"I don't know," Grandfather admitted sadly.

"Whenever I speak of him, everyone looks as if they already know he's dead. But they can't know that, can they? What if Father is trying to find us? We are not in Phnom Penh now, and not even in Cambodia. How will he know where to look when so many thousands have run away?"

Grandfather thought for a long time.

"It would be hard to find one girl among thousands," he said, and rubbed his lips with his thumb and forefinger. Then he smiled. "But how hard could it be to find one American photographer by the name of Seth Conway?"

He took Chantrea by the hand. "Come with me."

They passed family groups and children at play as they moved through the camp. Guards with rifles glanced at them, but Chantrea noticed they did not have the same cold stares as the guards at the rice camp. These men were here to protect her, she reminded herself.

Grandfather asked a few people where he might find Jack. One younger man pointed toward the entrance to the camp. Grandfather led Chantrea there. Jack stood by a truck with a clipboard in his hand, as he spoke to the driver. As they approached, the driver got out and went to the back of the truck. She opened the doors to reveal large boxes and barrels.

"Jack, may I speak with you?"

Jack turned around. A smile lit up his face. "Hello, Meng. Just got a shipment of food in. I'm sure glad to see it."

Chantrea's eyes rounded. All of that was food?

"Yes, you can believe your eyes," Jack said with a laugh. "I think we'll have some good eats at lunch today."

Grandfather looked from the truck to the clipboard to Jack's dark, smiling face.

"I interrupt you," he said.

"Not at all," Jack insisted. "What can I do for you?"

"My granddaughter, Chantrea," Grandfather said, "her father is an American. We hope you can help us find him. When we first came here, Tommy Fordham thought it was possible."

Jack nodded. "Yes, Tommy told me about him. From Ohio, right?"

Chantrea smiled. "Yes, sir. Ohio, America."

"Okay, tell you what," Jack said. "You let me finish this inventory, and get this food out to the other refugees. After lunch, we'll sit down and see how we can find your daddy for you. Okay, sweetheart?"

Chantrea's smile widened. "Okay!"

As they walked back to their tent, Chantrea felt so happy she thought she would burst. Suddenly, she didn't feel weak, or hungry. The pain in her legs and arms was gone. She would be with her father soon, and that was all that mattered.

Grandmother shared tea with another old woman. She was so thin now, after their long ordeal, that a shawl someone had donated to the camp wrapped around her twice. But Chantrea knew that Grandmother would soon be strong and well. Once Father came here, everything would change.

"Grandmother, I have wonderful news!" Chantrea cried.

"Chantrea, your manners," Grandmother scolded.

Quickly, Chantrea bowed to the older woman at her grandmother's side. The woman nodded at her but did not speak.

"Now, what is this news?"

Chantrea told her how Jack planned to contact Father for her. But instead of a smile, Grandmother looked up at Grandfather with a worried frown.

"This is what she was told, Meng?" Grandmother asked.

"Jack says he'll try," Grandfather replied.

Grandmother shock her head. "It is wrong to give a child false hopes."

"But they aren't false hopes, Grandmother," Chantrea insisted. She put her hand on the woman's shoulder, and felt a hard knob of bone there. "We'll find Father. I know we will!"

"Perhaps we should pray to Buddha tonight," Grandmother said.

The other woman spoke at last.

"My family has a little temple," she said. "You may pray there, if you'd like."

"Thank you," Grandmother said. She looked up at Chantrea.

"Thank you," Chantrea told the older woman and bowed again.

Chantrea and her grandparents found the little makeshift temple. It wasn't grand like the beautiful *wat* they visited in Phnom Penh, but the small statues of Buddha that had been brought here were surrounded by candles and beautiful flowers. Chantrea bent her head and prayed as hard as she could.

When they left the little tent, Chantrea saw children run by. Their laughter and shouts filled the air.

"What is happening?" Chantrea asked a boy.

"Food!" the boy cried. "Come get on line! The food truck is open!"

Chantrea looked at her grandparents.

"Go ahead, Chantrea," Grandfather said. "Get something good to eat."

And it *was* good. The vegetables over hot, steaming rice tasted better than anything Chantrea had eaten in her life. She closed her eyes and breathed in the wonderful aroma. She savored every delicious bite. When the rice and vegetables were gone, she used her fingers to wipe away every last trace. Then she went to find her grandparents. They sat with the other elders as they ate their own meals.

"Go play with the other children," Grandmother told her. "You have had a fine meal for the first time in months. It is time for you to act like a girl again."

Play? Chantrea had forgotten what the word meant. They never played at the rice farm. They worked, they listened to speeches, they slept. There were no toys, no dolls there. And Chantrea wasn't really certain she ever wanted to play with toys again.

"What . . . what should I do?" she asked.

Grandfather laughed. "Look around. I'm sure you can be clever."

Chantrea did look. She began to see that the children had all managed to find ways to entertain themselves. Three little girls gathered nearby with their rag dolls. Someone had stuffed rags into pieces of cloth and tied them off to make the doll's heads, then painted faces on them. The dolls were wrapped in old, ragged *kramas*. But the little girls loved them as if they had been bought at a fine booth in a market place. Little boys pushed trucks made from tin cans and buttons, or flew kites made from scraps of newspaper, string, and bamboo sticks. One child sailed a little boat in a mud puddle.

"Hey, you," said a voice.

Chantrea turned to see a boy, of about her own age, watching her. He tossed a ball up and down.

"You're new here?" he asked.

Chantrea nodded. "My name is Chantrea."

"I'm Kosal," the boy said. "Saw you by the food truck. You know anything about baseball?"

Chantrea grinned. "I love that game! My father taught me how to play."

"Jack taught me," Kosal said. "He gave me this baseball and this bat."

He called some of the other children, and within a few minutes a game began. Chantrea thought of the wonderful days in the park by her home in Phnom Penh, when her father had played with her. She remembered when he'd tried to teach Mother how to play. Mother had giggled so much that she could never catch the ball.

Suddenly, she thought she might cry again. But she bit her lip to stop herself. It was her turn on the pitcher's mound, a triangle marked off in the dirt with a stick. She wound up and threw the ball at Kosal. He missed it twice but struck it hard the third time and ran around the bases as his team shouted encouraging words. The bases were bits of torn bamboo mat, and home plate was an old *krama*. Kosal pounded onto the dirty, torn scarf. His bare feet sent up clouds of dust.

"Home run!" shouted another boy, speaking in Khmer.

When the game was over, Kosal walked over to Chantrea.

"You play pretty good," Kosal said. "Hey . . . what's the matter?"

"Nothing," Chantrea insisted.

"You look like you're gonna cry, or something," said Kosal.

Chantrea gave her head a rough shake. "No, I'm not."

Kosal shifted from one bare, dirty foot to the other. Then he thrust out his hand and offered Chantrea the baseball.

"You can hold this for a little while," he said.

"Thanks," Chantrea said, and took the ball. His little act of kindness touched her, and she couldn't stop a tear as it slid down her cheek. She wiped it away quickly.

"It's okay," Kosal said. "We all have things to be sad about. My father was killed by the Khmer Rouge. But I have my mother and my little brother."

"I lost my mother," Chantrea said. "My father is an American. Tommy and Jack are going to find him for me."

Kosal tilted his head. "American, huh?"

"Yes, he is," Chantrea said. Her eyes narrowed. Would Kosal say something bad now?

"That's cool," he said.

Chantrea laughed at the unexpected phrase.

"You use American words, like my father," she said. "Sometimes, my grandfather talks like that. It's funny."

"I learned it from Tommy," Kosal said.

"Tommy is really nice," Chantrea said. "A lot of people here are really nice."

"Yes, but it isn't home. Where are you from, anyway?"

"Phnom Penh," Chantrea told him.

"I'm from Siem Reap," Kosal said. "Hey, I hear my mother calling me. She probably wants me to do work in our garden."

"You have a garden?"

"A lot of people do," Kosal said. "That way, we have extra food for ourselves. You should try to plant one, too."

"I won't be here long enough to see it grow," Chantrea said.

Kosal turned to walk away. He looked back over his shoulder.

"I hope that's true!" he called.

Now Chantrea spotted Jack. He sat on a log with a bottle of Coke. She thought of a question and went to ask him.

"Hello, Chantrea," Jack said. "Want a soda?"

Chantrea shook her head. She had tasted it with her meal today, and thought it was too sweet.

"What's up?" Jack asked.

"When will you send a letter to my father?"

Jack laughed. "In a hurry, are you?"

But then he noticed the serious look on Chantrea's face and stopped laughing.

"Yeah, I guess you would be," he said. "I know I miss my own kids."

"You have children?"

"Well, they aren't little," Jack said. "My son is in college and my daughter works as a secretary. But I think about them a lot. My wife died a few years ago, so it's just my kids now."

"I only have my grandparents, and my father," said Chantrea.

Jack took a bandanna out of his pocket and wiped sweat from his forehead.

"It's a sin what those people did to your country," he said, "the way they kill people and break up families. If I can get you back with your dad, it would make me feel very good. The mail truck comes once a week, sweetheart. You can bet I'll have a letter on it next time it's around."

"When will that be?" Chantrea asked anxiously.

"In a day or two," Jack said. "You let me worry about that, okay? Just go on getting stronger and being a real kid again. God knows there's enough sick kids here."

He pointed to the ball that Chantrea held.

"I saw you play baseball," he said. "You're good at it, kid. You'll fit right in with any other American kid."

"Maybe my father will want to stay here when he comes for me," Chantrea said. "Maybe the Khmer Rouge will be driven out of my country, and we'll be able to live in Cambodia again."

Jack tipped back his soda bottle and finished the drink.

"I hope that's true, sweetheart," he said, with that same sad look Chantrea had seen on so many faces lately, "I hope that's true."

Chapter Eight

THE meals served from the food truck were delicious. Each time Chantrea ate, she had to remind herself this wasn't a dream. She didn't have to pretend watery gruel was fluffy, fragrant rice. She didn't have to try and remember the taste of vegetables and fish. It was real. And if her dreams of eating good food could come true, so could the dream that she would be with her father again.

The mail truck finally came, and Jack kept his promise to send out a letter. He showed Chantrea the blank envelope, with the letter inside.

"Do you know where your grandparents live in Ohio?" he asked Chantrea.

Chantrea shook her head. "I went there when I was seven, but I don't remember much. We were supposed to go there this past summer. But . . ."

"But you never got the chance, did you?" Jack said.

"Does that mean you can't send the letter?" Chantrea asked with worry.

"Not at all," Jack said. "You told me the name of his magazine, and that's where I'll send this. I'll ask them to forward it."

There was an old stone wall nearby. Jack leaned on it and wrote out the address. He only knew the magazine's name, and the town, but he was pretty certain it would get to the right people. Then he handed it to Chantrea.

"Here, sweetheart," he said. "You should be the one to post it."

Chantrea grinned and ran to the truck. It was a van that carried in supplies and mail and carried out letters home from the volunteers. Today, it would also help deliver Chantrea's own letter. And one day, when it came back, there would be a wonderful note from her father. He would promise to come right away.

Soon, the truck rumbled away, through the bamboo gateway of the compound and up the rough dirt road.

"How long will it take?" Chantrea asked.

"Now, you have to be patient," Jack said. "That letter has to get to a helicopter, and then to the airport in Bangkok. Then a long voyage across the Pacific and the United States, until it arrives in Ohio."

Chantrea frowned. She hadn't thought of the thousands of miles between here and Ohio. Jack put a big hand on her small, thin shoulder.

"Cheer up," he said. "You've waited this long. What's a few more weeks?"

Jack was right, and Chantrea did cheer up. For the first time in months, she finally had real hope. Someone had finally done something that would help her find her father.

"I will wait as patiently as I can," she said. "But you'll tell me when the answer comes?"

"The very second it arrives," Jack promised.

Now Kosal came up to her with several other children.

"Want to play baseball?" he asked. She nodded and smiled in reply.

They played the game under the pleasant morning sun.

Later, after she had finished her noon meal, Chantrea went back to her tent. It had grown very hot, but the light drizzle of rain helped to cool the air a little. Grandfather knelt on the dirt just outside the tent. He had drawn a square around himself with a stick, and marked off little, even rows. When Chantrea's shadow fell across the patch of dirt, he looked up.

"Hello, Chantrea," he said. "Look what I got from the truck today."

He held up three packets of seeds. One was labelled snow peas, one was for cucumbers, and another for squash.

"You're going to plant a garden, Grandfather?" Chantrea asked.

"Yes, it is time we did something for ourselves," Grandfather said. "We can't rely on the kindness of others to feed us forever."

"We won't have to, when Father comes," Chantrea said. "I mailed my letter today."

"Good for you," Grandfather said. "Would you like to help me plant these?"

Chantrea thought of how she'd told Kosal she wouldn't have time to watch a garden grow. But Grandfather seemed so happy to be busy. Even if they never saw a single vegetable, at least the garden could be passed on to someone else. New people came into the camp every week. This little garden could give one family hope.

"I would love to help you, Grandfather," Chantrea replied. She looked around them. "Where is Grandmother?"

"Resting inside," Grandfather said. "The heat gets to be too much for her."

He pointed to a pile of narrow bamboo sticks and a ball of string.

"I borrowed the string from one of the volunteers," he said. "Can you make me a trellis for the snow pea vines?"

Chantrea did so. She dug some holes on either side of the neat rows Grandfather had marked. Then she placed the bamboo sticks inside, deep enough so they wouldn't fall over. She tied three rows of strings between the two sticks. Then she repeated the task two more times. There were soon three trellises for the peas. But, Chantrea thought, someone else would see the curling vines wrap themselves around the string and poles. They would be gone by the time the plants grew tall.

"Good job, Chantrea," Grandfather said. He had planted all the seeds and had carefully covered them.

Now a group of children ran up to him. They were all wet from the steady light rain, but no one seemed to care.

"Grandfather Meng! Grandfather Meng!" they called.

Chantrea smiled to hear the little ones. Most of them

no longer had grandparents. With his kind ways and his warm smile, Grandfather had become a new grandparent to them. Two of the children were Nary's sisters, Dara and Kalliyan. Another little girl hugged Grandfather's legs. She was terribly thin and pale, but her dark eyes shone brightly. Chantrea knew she was one of the refugees who had come into the camp just recently. She looked down at her own arms and legs and saw that good food had started to put weight back on her body. It was only a matter of time before this frail little girl was as healthy and strong as the twins.

"Do some magic tricks for us, Grandfather Meng!" Kalliyan cried.

Grandfather laughed. "All right. Watch carefully."

For the next half hour, Grandfather entertained the children. He had managed to create props for his magic tricks from things he'd found around the camp. He was just like the children, Chantrea thought. He could make something from nothing the way they had made balls and dolls and toy trucks from rags and cans and buttons.

When Grandfather finished his little show, the children applauded. Some of the adults who stood nearby clapped, too. Then they gathered up the little ones. The day had grown almost unbearably hot, and it was time for naps. The woman who cared for the twins took each by the hand. Dara and Kalliyan protested that they were not tired, even though they both yawned noisily.

"It's best that we lay down, too," Grandfather said. "It's a very hot day today."

So they rested inside their tents, as men stood guard in the watchtowers and volunteers went about their business of caring for almost a thousand people. The rain fell heavier now, and lulled Chantrea to sleep. When she woke up an hour later, she went outside. Nary had just returned. She had a sad look on her face, and tears in her eyes.

"What's wrong, Nary?"

"It's a little boy we brought in two days ago," Nary said. "He can't be more than three. He seems to have no family."

"Surely someone will adopt him," Chantrea said.

"There are so many orphaned children," Nary said. "I don't know if we can find families for all of them. But that isn't why I'm crying. We . . . I mean the doctor . . . tried to put an IV into his arm."

"An IV?" Chantrea asked.

"That means intravenous," Nary explained. "You put a tube into someone's vein and feed them nourishment and medicine. But this little boy is as frail as a pile of thin bamboo sticks. It took us twenty minutes to find a place that would hold the needle, and even then half of it poked out of him."

Chantrea thought of the bamboo sticks she'd used in Grandfather's garden. Could a baby's arms and legs be that thin? Babies were supposed to be fat. Once again, she cursed the Khmer Rouge and what they had done.

Nary began to cry. "I keep thinking of those beautiful eyes, staring up at me. He doesn't talk, but I knew what his eyes said. They asked me, 'Why? Why?' And I couldn't answer."

"No one could answer," Chantrea told her, and hugged her in a show of comfort.

96

"Nary, let me help you tomorrow," Chantrea said. "Please. I'm so much better now. I've mailed a letter to America, and Jack says it will be some time before I get an answer. Let me keep busy helping the doctors and nurses."

"Well, you're only thirteen . . ."

"I'll be fourteen in a few months," Chantrea said. "I can help! And I'm not a little child anymore."

Now Nary smiled. "I know you aren't. But you can't be prepared for what you will see in that tent. You've only played with the healthy, lucky children. It will be a great shock to see the others."

"I don't mind," Chantrea insisted.

"All right, then," Nary said. "I'll talk to Dr. Lawrence tomorrow and see what you can do. Even if it is only to sit and hold a child's hand in your own."

———

THE next morning, after breakfast, Nary came up to Chantrea.

"You can come with me today," she said. "Dr. Lawrence says it's okay. He says that surely you've seen things as bad as what's in the hospital tents . . . and even worse."

Now Chantrea felt a little scared. How bad was it? She'd seen people brought in on stretchers, but not up close. She'd heard screams and howls of pain throughout the day and night.

But, she reminded herself, she had also seen many dead people. Back at the rice camp, she had seen victims of starvation and disease. During their trek out of Cambodia, she had seen skeletons picked clean by crows and vultures. What could be worse? she asked herself. She could be strong now. She was almost grownup.

It was the smell of the first tent that shocked her, and made her want to turn and run. But Nary held on to her.

"You'll get used to it, I promise," she said. "Here, put this on."

Nary gave her a mask, and helped her tie it around her face. Then she led her up to Dr. Lawrence.

"This is Chantrea Conway," she said.

"Conway, huh?" the doctor repeated. "That's an American name."

"My father is American," Chantrea said, and tried not to make a face because of the bad smell. "He is going to come back for me. I sent him a letter."

"Good for you," Dr. Lawrence said.

Dr. Lawrence spoke with a British accent. He had light brown hair with feathery bangs that fell into his green eyes. He had a mustache, just like Father had, and a beard, too.

"Well, we can surely use any help we can get," the doctor said. "Chantrea, the nurses are just about done feeding the patients. Those that can eat from a spoon, that is. Can you help them gather up the dishes?"

"Yes, I can!" Chantrea said, eager to show she could help.

She went up to a young woman with long blonde hair tied back in a ponytail, who said her name was Rachel. Rachel told her what to do, and Chantrea went to work. She tried not to look at the thin, wasted patients, but she could not stop herself. So many starving, sick people! And right now the leader of the Khmer Rouge, Pol Pot, probably sat at a fine meal in his own home. He probably didn't give one thought to his poor citizens.

A young boy tried to grab hold of her wrist. He looked like he was a few years older than Chantrea, but who could tell? He had the thin face of an old, old man and the small frame of a child. The legs that stretched out of a pair of shorts were nothing but bones wrapped in scabby, bandaged skin.

"Hello," he said in a weak voice. "Who are you?"

"My name is Chantrea."

"My . . . my name is Arun. Can you sit with me?"

"I have to pick up dishes."

Rachel heard this, and took the pile of bowls from Chantrea's hands.

"I'll do that," she said. "You can keep Arun company. It's more important."

So Chantrea sat at the edge of the bed. She suddenly realized she didn't smell the bad odor now. She had already gotten used to it.

"Where are you from, Chantrea?" Arun asked in a soft voice.

"Phnom Penh," she said.

His eyes, so big in his thin face, widened.

"Really? So am I! Where did you live?"

Chantrea told him, and explained that her father was an American. "He's a photographer," she said.

"I remember him," Arun said, to Chantrea's surprise. "He always had three or four cameras around his neck, and he drove a little blue car. A Beetle, I think?"

99

"Yes, yes, that's true," Chantrea said. She was delighted to meet someone from her own home. "Did you . . . did you leave the city when they made everyone go?"

"Yes, I was one of the thousands," Arun said. "They shot my parents. My uncle took care of me then. We had to dig ditches, for hours and hours every day. But we found a way to escape, and here we are."

"Where is your uncle?"

Arun sighed so deeply his whole body shook.

"Dead," he said. "He stepped on a land mine. I . . . I found my way here on my own. One day, I just collapsed on the jungle floor. Someone picked me up and brought me here. I don't know who."

Chantrea thought of the way Tommy and Jack had rescued them at the border.

"How long have you been here?"

"I don't know," Arun said. "A week or two, maybe. Dr. Lawrence says I'm getting stronger every day. I can even feed myself now."

"That's good news," Chantrea said.

She suddenly felt very, very lucky. Somehow, she had survived the last months with only a few scratches and mosquito bites. She hadn't gotten sick, and had only lost two teeth. When Arun showed her his weak smile, he was missing most of his, and what teeth were left were yellow.

"You will get better," she insisted. She held out her arm. "I was so skinny when I came here, but the food is good and I'm getting fatter again."

"They only let me eat clear broth and plain rice now," Arun said, "but soon, I'll get something more to eat. As soon as I can keep it down."

He suddenly began to cough. Chantrea stood up quickly. She thought he was about to throw up. But he soon calmed down.

"My lungs hurt a lot," he said. "I think I'd like to sleep now. Chantrea, will you come back and talk to me again tomorrow?"

"Yes, I will," Chantrea said with a smile. "We can talk about Phnom Penh and see if we knew any of the same people."

But when she went back the next day, Arun's bed was empty.

"He died last night," Rachel explained. "He had pneumonia, and his body could not take the stress."

Chantrea stood there, shocked, and suddenly her body shook with sobs, but it wasn't just for Arun. It was for Piarun and Chantou and so many others.

Nary put an arm over Chantrea's shoulders.

"Don't cry," she said. "You helped to make his last moments happy, Chantrea."

Chantrea nodded. Even though she'd known Arun for a short while, she felt grief-stricken. How many more would die? she wondered. How many more would suffer because of a madman named Pol Pot and his evil troops?

Chapter Nine

THERE were three hospital tents in the compound.
The victims of starvation were cared for separately
from those who had been hurt by bullets or land mines or
bombs. Those with diseases were housed in the third tent.
Nary explained that only the doctors and nurses were allowed in there.

Over the next weeks, Chantrea spent all of her vol-
unteer time in the tent with the people who had almost
died of hunger. She was heartbroken to see the way they
gazed at her with big, empty eyes. Some of them were so
weak they could not even tell their names, or where they
had come from.

"What's wrong, Chantrea?" Grandfather asked one
day. "Ever since you began to work in the hospital tent,
you don't smile as much."

"I feel so sorry for them all, Grandfather," Chantrea

cried. "Do you think this will ever end? Do you think our people can ever be happy again?"

"I don't know, Chantrea," Grandfather said. "Perhaps, someday."

He smiled a little. "Our vegetables have sprouted. Would you like to see?"

"Yes, Grandfather," Chantrea said, but she still didn't smile.

Indeed, the rows Grandfather had marked off were now dotted with little green plants. Soon, the snow pea vines would begin to curl up over the trellis Chantrea had built. But she didn't want to be here when it happened. She wanted to leave Thailand and all the horror behind.

"Grandfather, when will Father come?"

Grandfather just sighed. "You ask that almost every day, Chantrea. And you know I don't have the answer."

"I'm going to the gate to see if the mail truck comes today," Chantrea said, and walked away.

But the mail truck did not come that day, nor the next. Jack spotted her and told her to be patient.

"I don't want to be patient," Chantrea retorted. "It's more than six months since I saw my father."

Jack started to say something, but Chantrea scowled at him. She felt angry, and she was tired of people who thought her dream to see her father was a waste of time. So Jack simply walked away. Chantrea sat on a rock and stared at the closed, locked bamboo gates. She listened for the sound of the mail truck's engine. But she only heard the voices of a thousand people and the noises of the surrounding jungle.

For the next days, Chantrea followed the same routine, rain or shine. After a breakfast of rice and milk, she went with Nary to the tent. When her work was done, Kosal tried to get her to play, but she refused. How could she play when so many were so sick?

Each afternoon, she sat on the rock near the gate and watched for the truck. Even when the monsoon rains fell on her, she did not move. Finally, Grandmother had had enough.

"You must stop this, Chantrea," she insisted. "It is not good for a young girl to make herself so upset!"

"Others need me, Grandmother," Chantrea said. "I have no right to be happy and healthy. Who am I to be so lucky?"

"Who are you to question why Buddha does what he does?" Grandmother asked. "Yes, you are lucky. Be glad of it. It is not your fault what happened to those others."

Chantrea felt her lower lip begin to quiver. Soon, her tears fell. Grandmother put a hand on her shoulder.

"It will be all right, Chantrea," she said. "Your dreams will come true one day."

"Do you really believe that?" Chantrea asked.

Grandmother had been one of those who thought Father would never return.

"Yes, I do," Grandmother said quietly. After a moment, she said: "Chantrea, I don't want you to go back to that hospital tent."

"But . . ."

"Do not argue with me," Grandmother said. "I have already spoken to Nary, and she agrees. You are too young to see all the things you've seen. No more work for you."

Chantrea could tell by Grandmother's tone that she

could not argue. In a way, she was relieved. It was hard work, even the little she did, and she was tired. But she would not let Grandmother, or anyone else, tell her she couldn't watch for the mail truck.

Then, finally, a letter came from Father's magazine, addressed to Jack. Chantrea wondered why it didn't come from her American grandparents' house. Why didn't Father write?

"Don't fret so much," Chantrea told herself. "He wrote it when he was at his office!"

But she could not stop worrying. After all this time, she suddenly felt very afraid of what the letter might say. What if Grandmother and the others had been right? What if the letter told her Father was dead?

"No, I won't believe it!" Chantrea cried.

One of the soldiers up in the nearby guard tower leaned over to look down at her. Chantrea ignored him. She ran through the compound until she found Jack.

"Read this to me!" she begged. "Please?"

"Chantrea, I know you can read English," Jack said.

"Please, I'm scared of what it says," Chantrea admitted.

Jack took the envelope and opened it. He skimmed over the letter for a moment, and frowned.

"What is it?" Chantrea asked. "What's wrong? Is it my father? He's dead, isn't he? Isn't he?"

"No, he's alive," Jack said.

Chantrea let out a long sigh of relief. But before she could say how happy she was, Jack added, "Chantrea, there is good news and bad news in this letter. Come over here and sit down with me while I read it."

They sat on a pair of folding chairs, and Jack began to read.

Dear Mr. VanBuren:

"*We received your letter today regarding Seth Conway. We are very sorry to hear of his daughter's situation and hope we can help.*

"*Please tell Chantrea that her father came back to America shortly after the city of Phnom Penh was invaded. He told us he had tried every means of getting back to his family, but could not find them among the thousands of refugees spread across the country. He was forced to leave Cambodia. But he made plans to return as quickly as he could, to continue his search for his family. He left a month ago and we have not heard from him.*"

Chantrea gasped. Why hadn't Father's friends heard from him in a month's time?

"Easy, Chantrea," Jack said. "Let me finish."

He went on:

"*In the meantime, we have forwarded your letter to Chantrea's grandparents, Joseph and Laura Conway. We're helping them make arrangements to bring her to America, where she can wait in safety for her father's return. They have also invited her Cambodian grandparents to be their guests as long as they wish to stay in America. We are certain Seth will soon*"

*be in touch with his daughter, and he will be over-
joyed to know she is found, and safe.*

*"We have also sent word out to all possible
sources to be on the lookout for Chantrea's father.
They will relay a message that Chantrea is currently
at your camp.*

*"We hope that Seth and his daughter will soon
be reunited. We only regret that their reunion will not
include Chantrea's mother. Words can't express our
sorrow at the Conway family's loss, nor can we imagine the horrors Chantrea and her fellow Cambodians
have faced.*

*"Please let us know if there is anything else we
can do for the little girl. We are all very fond of Seth
here and look forward to meeting his daughter."*

Jack read the signature, then looked up.

"Chantrea?"

Chantrea stared thoughtfully down the pathway that
ran between two rows of huts.

"Father is here somewhere, looking for me," she said.
"But where? In Cambodia, or Thailand?"

"Chantrea, your grandparents want you in America,"
Jack said.

She looked at him. "I don't want to go to America. I
want to stay here until Father comes!"

"But, Chantrea, that could take a long time," Jack
said. "At least, if you are in America, you will be safe. And
your father is certain to write to your American grandparents. He will know to come home."

Chantrea thought about this and realized Jack was right. And she really did want to get far away from here.

"What will my Cambodian grandparents say?"

"I hope they will agree it is the best thing to do."

They brought the letter to Grandfather. He read it carefully and said. "Yes, this is what we must do. I have considered it for a long time. Can you make the arrangements, Jack?"

"I'll see to it right away, Meng," Jack promised. He smiled at Chantrea. "Keep your chin up, sweetheart. Who knows? Maybe by the time we get all the visas for you, your father will be here!"

But that did not happen. Even though it took several weeks to get their papers, there was no sign of Father. By then, Chantrea was very eager to go to America. She knew Father would find her more easily there than here. Still, she was sad to leave the friends she had made. They all gathered to say good-bye to the Mok family.

"Nary, you were like a big sister to me," she told her friend. "I hope that one day you will dance again."

"I will think of you whenever I do," Nary promised.

Tears streamed down their eyes as they hugged. Chantrea moved away and went to Kosal.

"I'm not gonna hug you," Kosal said, "and I'm not gonna cry!"

He sounded so tough, so much older than fourteen. But he did hug Chantrea, and his eyes were wet when he pulled away.

"Have fun playing baseball in America," he said.

She said good-bye to Jack and Tommy and all the

other friends she had made. Dara and Kalliyan tugged on Grandfather's shirt.

"Do one more magic trick for us, Grandfather Meng!" they begged in unison.

Grandfather pulled a coin out from behind Dara's ear, and then another from Kalliyan's. The little twins giggled.

"It's time to go now," Tommy said.

He would drive them to the bus station, where they would take a bus to Bangkok. There, they would take the first step of a long journey to America. They climbed into the car. Chantrea opened her window and leaned out to wave at her friends. Everyone called good-bye. Chantrea saw Jack wipe his eyes with a red bandana.

"Well, here we go," Tommy said.

They drove for a while through the jungle. Chantrea had heard that there were troops hiding in there, but she saw no sign of them. Soon, they came to a little clearing with a single bamboo hut. An old run-down bus waited nearby.

"Now, you're sure you have all your papers?" Tommy asked.

"Quite sure," Grandfather said, and patted the buttoned pocket of his khaki-colored shirt.

"I'll ride the bus to the airport with you," Tommy said. "And I'll make sure you get on the airplane all right."

"Thank you, Tommy," Grandfather said.

They boarded the bus together. Chantrea was surprised to see so many others waiting there. Soon, the bus was filled with other refugees. Chantrea gazed out the window. She felt both excited and scared. She saw an argument take place between a man and a woman. The woman did not want to go on the bus. She told the man she did not want to leave her loved ones behind. Finally, the man agreed to stay with her. But he looked unhappy, and Chantrea knew he had truly wanted to leave.

At last, the bus began to roll. It bumped and joggled over the rough dirt roads. For the next twelve hours, the refugees made their way to Bangkok. They took only two rest stops. Once, they had to wait for a gaggle of geese to walk in front of the bus. By the time they reached the airport, it was the middle of the night. Chantrea was deep asleep.

"Come on, honey," Tommy said, as he gently shook her awake. "Your big adventure is about to begin."

They all shuffled off the bus, and Chantrea noticed there were several other buses parked right behind their own. Ragged people like herself, their eyes wide and frightened, were organized into a line. They marched into the airport. Chantrea thought of the day they had marched onto the rice farm back in Cambodia. Everyone then had had the same frightened looks on their faces. But today, she saw something else. There were a few smiles, a few expressions of wonder. Maybe it was scary to leave the world you knew, Chantrea thought, but it was exciting to think of a new life in a strange, new place!

"What will happen now, Tommy?" Grandfather asked.

"They'll look over your papers," Tommy explained, "and you'll wait for a flight. It might take a few hours; there are a lot of people here."

Chantrea looked around the terminal. She now saw that there were many more people than just the refugees.

There were people dressed in nice clothes, and children who looked happy and well fed. Chantrea thought some of the children might be going to see grandparents, too. But they were not trying to escape a life of sorrow. One girl, who looked about nine, stared at the ragged group with an open mouth. Her mother said something and pulled her away. Just before she turned, her eyes fell on Chantrea. Chantrea smiled. The younger girl gave her a little smile back, and then disappeared into the crowd of people waiting for their flights.

Chantrea thought the airport was the busiest place she had ever seen, even busier than downtown Phnom Penh. Tommy told her she could look out the window as the planes took off.

"Grandmother, Grandfather?" Chantrea said. "Would you like to come look with me?"

"I'll stay here on the line," Grandfather said with a smile.

Grandmother shuddered. "I want no part of those big metal birds!"

Chantrea went to the window. She'd never seen an airplane parked on the ground before. There had been many that flew over Phnom Penh, some of them commercial craft and some military. Up in the sky, they did look as Grandmother had described them: like big metal birds. The jumbo jet sat quietly on the tarmac now, shining in the bright lights. In a short time, she would be inside and flying away.

But it wasn't a short time at all before they were allowed to board the plane. Hours went by, and the group grew tired and impatient as the sky outside grew pink with dawn's light. Their papers were checked again and again, until Chantrea began to feel they would all be rejected and sent back to the refugee camp. She thought of the nice meals of rice and vegetables they'd eaten there. Her stomach growled and her head felt funny.

"Well, this is it," Tommy said suddenly.

"This is what, Tommy?" Grandfather asked.

"They're boarding passengers now," Tommy said. "You're on your way."

He held out a hand and Grandfather gave it a hard shake.

"Good luck to you, Mok Meng," Tommy said.

He turned to Chantrea and gave her a hug. "Next summer, you keep an eye on the Reds and write and tell me about their season."

"Okay, Tommy," Chantrea said with a grateful smile for the man who had done so much for them. She knew the Cincinnati Reds were one of Tommy's favorite baseball teams.

Tommy gave Grandmother a hug, but the old woman said nothing. Tears streamed down her face.

"Will you be all right, Teva?" Tommy asked.

"I am frightened," Grandmother said, "but I will do what I have to do."

At last, they showed their tickets to the stewardess and walked out to the plane. As Chantrea climbed the metal steps, her heart suddenly began to pound. Tommy had said her big adventure was about to begin. She thought of her happy life in Phnom Penh, the forced march out of the city, the months of hunger and pain at the rice farm. She thought of her mother, of Piarun, of Nary. Suddenly, it all seemed like the life a different girl had led, not Chantrea Conway.

What, she wondered, would her new life in America be like?

Chapter Ten

CHANTREA felt strange when the airplane left the
ground, almost as if the world had dropped away
from her. Grandmother give a little startled cry. She sat
in the middle of three seats, with Grandfather on the aisle
and Chantrea at the window. Chantrea knew that Grandmother was afraid, and she was a little scared herself. But
it was fun, too, to imagine there was nothing but air beneath them!

A stewardess came out and talked to the passengers
about safety. She told them that oxygen masks would fall
from the ceiling if the cabin pressure changed. That made
Grandmother grab Grandfather's arm and squeeze it
hard.

"Why do they have those if this thing is safe, Meng?"
she demanded.

"All will be well, Teva," Grandfather insisted.

"I will pray for us," Grandmother said, and closed her eyes.

Grandfather leaned forward a bit to see Chantrea, and asked, "How about you? Are you afraid?"

"Just a little," Chantrea admitted. "But it's a good kind of afraid."

Grandfather nodded. They had all known fear these past months. Flying thousands of feet in the air was nothing compared to hiding in a jungle for six weeks, running from armed soldiers!

Chantrea soon heard a rattling noise, as the stewardesses wheeled the food cart down the aisle. She had been so excited about the flight she had forgotten how hungry she was. The food tasted good to her. With her stomach full, she grew tired again. The humming engines were like a lullaby, and soon she was fast asleep.

Some time later, she woke up to see the stewardess pulling a white screen down in front of the plane. The lights were dimmed and soon a movie began to roll. Chantrea enjoyed watching the story of a little dog named Benji. She even laughed at a few parts. It was nice to forget her troubles, if only for a little while.

When the movie was over, she looked out her window but saw only clouds.

"When we will reach America?" she asked Grandfather.

"I don't know," he said. "Why don't you ask the stewardess?"

Chantrea remembered the call button on her seat from her last airplane trip to America. She pressed it and a chime summoned the stewardess.

116

"Yes, dear?" the pretty young woman asked with a smile.

"How many more hours until we reach America?"

"Oh, I'd say seven or eight," the stewardess replied. "And may I say, your English is excellent."

"Thank you," Chantrea said. "My father is from Ohio."

Even though she hadn't seen her father in months, these last few hours seemed the hardest of all. Time seemed to stretch as far and wide as the Pacific Ocean down below. Even dinner didn't make it go faster.

"You should try to sleep again, Chantrea," Grandmother said.

"I'm not tired," Chantrea said.

Grandfather called the stewardess again, and asked for a deck of cards. He passed the time with Chantrea playing games her father had taught them.

"Why does it have to be such a long way?" Chantrea asked.

"And yet, is it as long as the journey we took from Phnom Penh?" Grandfather asked.

At last, the pilot announced that they were approaching San Francisco. Chantrea almost burst with excitement. They were almost there! Soon, she'd see Father's family. And it would only be a few days before they found Father and she was with him again.

The plane landed so smoothly Chantrea didn't even know they were on the ground until she looked out her window. It taxied to position and came to a halt. Passengers stood up and began to gather their things. Chantrea never thought she'd seen people move more slowly.

"Stop dancing back and forth, Chantrea," Grandmother ordered.

"She's just eager to see Seth's family, Teva," Grandfather said.

They finally disembarked and walked down the staircase outside the plane. They crossed the tarmac with the other passengers and entered the terminal, where they waited in a line for customs inspection. When it was her turn, Chantrea proudly showed the inspector papers that proved her American citizenship.

"You've come a long way, little girl," he said with a smile.

"I'm here to see my father's family," Chantrea told him.

"Welcome to the United States of America," he said.

"Thank you," Chantrea said, almost in a whisper. After eight months, after thousands of miles, it still didn't seem real that she was here, in her father's homeland.

"What do we do now?" she asked her grandparents, "Where do we go?"

"Jack said someone would be waiting for us," Grandfather said. "But there are so many people here!"

A man approached them. He looked so much like Father that Chantrea knew at once this must be her Uncle Bill. She smiled up at him.

"Hello, Chantrea," he said. "You've made it here at last. Do you remember me?"

Chantrea made a polite little bow. "Yes, I remember you. Please, meet my grandparents, too."

"Hello," Grandfather said with a bow. "I am Mok Meng. This is my wife, Teva."

"Welcome to America, Meng," Uncle Bill said. "Welcome, Teva."

Grandmother gave him a tired smile. Now he held out his arm and an older woman stepped forward. Chantrea remembered her grandma Laura.

"Oh, thank God you're here!" Grandma Laura cried, and took Chantrea into a warm embrace. The smell of her perfume, like a thousand lotus blossoms, seemed to wrap around Chantrea like a cloud.

"Hello, Grandmother," Chantrea said. She wasn't sure what else to say, and suddenly felt a little scared.

"Call me Grandma Laura," she said. "That's what you did when you were little." She held Chantrea's face between two hands that were soft and cool. "Oh, it is so good to have you here, safe and sound."

She kept an arm around Chantrea's thin shoulders and smiled at Grandmother and Grandfather.

"How do you do?" she asked. "I'm Laura Conway, Seth's mother. I'm so pleased to meet you."

"As we are to meet you," Grandfather said.

Grandmother greeted her in Cambodian.

"My wife speaks little English," Grandfather explained.

Grandma Laura grinned. "That's all right. I can translate her smile easily enough!"

Now Uncle Bill gently pushed two kids in front of him. One was a girl who seemed a little older than Chantrea. She had light brown hair cut into feathery layers, and wore blue eye shadow. The other was a little boy with blond hair and hazel eyes. Chantrea saw at once that they were the same color as her father's eyes.

119

"Say hi to your cousin, kids," Uncle Bill said.

"Hi, do you remember me?" Kathy asked.

Chantrea really didn't remember her much. She looked very different now, six years later. But she did remember how nice Kathy had been, and smiled.

"Hello, Cousin Kathy," she said.

"Just Kathy, okay?" her cousin replied. "And this is my little brother, Jamie."

Jamie just giggled and hid his smile behind his hand.

"Jamie was just a baby when you last visited us," Grandma Laura said.

"He's almost seven now," Kathy said. "Don't pay any attention to him if he gets silly. You can sit next to me in the van, okay?"

"Okay," Chantrea smiled. She suddenly recalled something from her last visit. "Kathy, do you still have that big pink bear that used to sit in your room?"

Kathy laughed. "You remember that? Yes, he's still there. But there's a lot of different stuff, too."

"And if we don't get moving here," Uncle Bill said, "she'll never see it."

Chantrea looked around.

"Where is my grandfather Conway?" she asked. "Will I see him today?"

"Unfortunately, Dad wasn't well enough to travel," Uncle Bill explained. "We've got a little ways to go before we get to Ohio, Chantrea. Another three thousand miles."

Grandmother said something in Cambodian.

"Excuse me?" Grandma Laura asked.

"My wife says she is tired of traveling," Grandfather translated.

"Of course she is," Grandma Laura said. "And here we stand in the middle of an airport, talking! Let's get your luggage and go."

"We . . . we have no luggage," said Grandfather with a sad shake of his head. "There was nothing to bring. Everything we owned . . . we had to leave it behind when the soldiers came to our city."

"Soldiers? Cool!" Jamie said.

"Oh, no, Jamie," Bill said to his son. "Those were bad soldiers."

"We should not talk of them," Grandfather insisted.

"You don't have to worry," Uncle Bill said. "You're in America now. You can speak freely here."

Grandma Laura gave his arm a little tug.

"Billy, if we don't get to the hotel, they'll fall asleep right here in the terminal."

"Okay, Mom," Bill agreed, and led them away.

At the doors, Grandma Laura stopped the group. She had been carrying a large shopping bag, and now she reached into it to produce three jackets. One was for Chantrea and the others for her grandparents.

"Our church donated these," Grandma Laura said. "We almost forgot you were coming from a very hot place into cool November weather! I hope they fit."

Chantrea slipped her jacket on. It was made of something that felt like leather. It crossed in front and tied with a belt. She ran her hands over the furry collar.

"Thank you . . . it's beautiful," she said. Chantrea had never even seen such a coat before.

Grandfather and Grandmother were also full of thanks.

Outside, everyone piled into a van. It wasn't like the run-down vehicles Chantrea had known in Cambodia and Thailand. It was clean and new, and very comfortable. Uncle Bill drove them to a hotel.

"We're going to spend the night," he said, "and then we'll start across the country in the morning."

Uncle Bill checked them in, then led the group upstairs.

"We rented adjoining rooms," Uncle Bill said as he unlocked one of the doors. "Chantrea, would you prefer to share with your grandparents?"

"Oh, can't she stay with me, Dad?" Kathy begged. "Please?"

Chantrea looked at her grandfather for approval. He smiled and nodded.

"You stay with your cousin, Chantrea," Grandfather said. "You need to be with other children after all these hours with old people."

Chantrea laughed. "You aren't old, Grandfather. But thank you—I do want to spend more time with Kathy."

"I'll stay with the children," Grandma Laura said.

Uncle Bill opened the door between the rooms. Jamie ran to one of the beds and claimed it as his own.

"Well, you'll share with me," Grandma Laura said. "The girls can have the bed by the window."

"I like mine better," Jamie declared. "It's right in front of the television."

"Do you have television in Cambodia, Chantrea?" Kathy asked.

Chantrea shook her head. "We never had a television.

122

We listened to the radio a lot. I mean, before the Khmer Rouge . . ."

She stopped, afraid that thoughts of those awful days would make her cry.

"Kathy, why don't you walk with Chantrea to the pop machine we passed?" Grandma Laura suggested.

"I want a pop, too!" Jamie insisted.

"Bring one back for your brother," Grandma Laura said, and gave Kathy some quarters.

In the hall, Kathy asked, "Do you like America, so far?"

"Oh, it is wonderful," Chantrea exclaimed. "I did not see one single soldier yet."

"Are there a lot of soldiers in Cambodia?"

"They are everywhere," Chantrea said. "At the rice camp, where we had to work, they stood guard."

"Gee, that must have been scary," Kathy said, shaking her head.

"I don't want to talk about the soldiers," Chantrea said. Just thinking about them was making her stomach tighten into knots.

"Sure, okay," Kathy agreed.

They reached the soda machine and Kathy plugged in the quarters.

"Do you go to school, Kathy?" Chantrea asked.

"Sure," Kathy said. "I'm only fourteen. I don't graduate for a few years yet."

"I want to go to school, too," Chantrea declared. It had been so long since she'd even read a book, and she'd never had a class taught in English, but she knew she'd enjoy it if the other kids were as friendly as Kathy.

Kathy handed her a soda, and she pulled the tab off.

"You will," Kathy said. "You'll be in the junior high. I'm in high school, myself. They let me take a few days off to come get you."

"I'm glad you came. You're even nicer than I remember," Chantrea said. Then she thought of something. "Kathy, where is your mother?"

"She died a few years ago," Kathy said in a quiet voice. "She was very sick."

"The soldiers killed my mother," Chantrea said.

"Then we both don't have mothers," Kathy replied.

They were quiet for a moment, sharing their sadness. But then, Jamie came running down the hall.

"Hey! Where's my pop?" he demanded.

Kathy rolled her eyes, and Chantrea giggled at her expression.

"Here you go, pest," Kathy said, and handed Jamie a 7UP. She looked at Chantrea. "Just be glad you don't have an annoying little brother."

She put her arm over Chantrea's shoulders and they went back to the room together.

That night, Grandmother and Grandfather insisted on sleeping on top of the bed, without the covers. After saying good-night to them Chantrea went into her own room. She felt strange climbing in next to Kathy. She had not had a thick, comfortable mattress to sleep on since April. The bed was so soft it was hard for her to get used to it, but somehow she fell fast asleep.

The next morning, she lay awake for a long time, staring at the ceiling.

"Are you okay, dear?" Grandma Laura asked.

Chantrea nodded and wiped away a tear that trickled from the corner of her eye.

"I was just listening to the quiet, Grandma Laura," she said.

"It ain't quiet in here," Jamie said. "The TV is on!"

"Shh, Jamie," Kathy said. She sat at the vanity, fussing with lipstick.

Grandma Laura sat on the bed and took Chantrea's hand in her own.

"What do you mean, Chantrea?"

"It is so nice to sleep a whole night and not wonder if an airplane is going to fly overhead and drop a bomb on you."

"Oh!" Grandma Laura gasped. She pulled Chantrea into her arms. "Put those awful thoughts from your mind, dear! You don't ever have to think of them again!"

She gave her granddaughter a kiss and stood up. "Now, get dressed and come on down to the restaurant. They serve a wonderful buffet breakfast here."

She left the room, taking Jamie with her. Chantrea started to put on the same clothes as the day before. She saw that Kathy had a fresh new outfit and wondered if her cousin had a lot of clothes. She began to realize how ragged her own clothes were. But still, they were better than the torn jeans and T-shirt she'd had on when they escaped from the rice farm!

Kathy was brushing her hair now. In the reflection, she saw Chantrea watching her from the bed. She turned around.

"You know what?" she said. "I bet I have something you can wear today. Okay?"

"Okay," Chantrea said with a smile. "I'd like to wear something that is yours."

Kathy poked around her suitcase and pulled out a pair of slacks and a shirt with wide, bell-like sleeves. Chantrea dressed while they chatted.

"You have pretty clothes," she said. She looked in the mirror and admired the shirt, which was made of a light, crinkled fabric and embroidered with many colors.

"You look great," Kathy said. "I'm hungry, aren't you?"

Chantrea nodded. They hurried downstairs to the hotel's restaurant.

"Grandma Laura," Kathy said, "can we get Chantrea some clothes when we get to Columbus?"

"You bet," Grandma Laura said.

A long table was set up with more food than Chantrea had ever seen in her life. Her grandparents ate mostly fruits, but Chantrea tasted a little of everything. It was all so delicious she thought she might start crying again. Her dream was slowly coming true, and if this was just the beginning she could only imagine how wonderful life would be in America.

And when she was finally reunited with her father, it would be perfect.

Chapter Eleven

IT was a long drive from San Francisco to Ohio, but
Chantrea was glad to see some of her father's country.
Uncle Bill told her the name of each state as they passed
through: California, Nevada, Utah, and more. Sometimes,
Jamie got fidgety, but Chantrea couldn't get enough of the
scenery that flew by the van. In Wyoming, Grandmother
complained that she was too cold, despite the coat she
wore, but none of the Conways understood her Khmer
speech. Grandfather cheerfully translated for them. Unlike Grandmother, he was as fascinated by everything
that was new as Chantrea was.

Late in the evening of the second day, they stopped
to eat at a small restaurant in Iowa. Even though it was
only early November, a light snow had already begun to
fall. Grandma Laura suddenly noticed the sandal-clad feet
of Chantrea and her grandparents.

"Oh, dear!" she cried. "I thought about coats—but completely forgot about shoes. You can't wear those open sandals at this time of year!"

And so, after lunch, they found a shoe store. Chantrea giggled as her bare feet were measured. Uncle Bill told the shoe salesman that his niece had just arrived from Cambodia. The man smiled up at her.

"You're a long way from home," he said.

Chantrea realized she had traveled almost halfway around the world in the last few days.

Grandma Laura bought her a pair of sneakers, and promised to get something more dressy when they arrived in Ohio. Chantrea, who had never worn shoes in her life, thought the soft canvas sneakers were just fine.

"My feet feel as if they are bound," Grandmother said, as she looked down at her own shoes. "Like the ladies of old China."

"Are they all right, Teva?" Grandma Laura asked the other woman, even though they couldn't understand each other.

"She says they are fine," Grandfather replied.

Chantrea smiled. She knew Grandfather was too polite to reveal Grandmother's true words.

They drove on for many more hours. Sometimes, Uncle Bill played music on the radio. Chantrea imagined her own father listening to songs like this, perhaps even singing along. Father had a wonderful voice.

"Look! Look!" Jamie cried suddenly. "There's the sign for Ohio!"

"Just a few more hours," Uncle Bill said.

Finally, they reached Columbus and pulled into the

driveway of a large brick house. For a moment, all Chantrea's grandparents could do was stand and stare. They had never seen such a big private home! Grandmother asked Grandfather if this was a government building.

"I do not want to see anyone from the government," she insisted.

"It is their home, Grandmother," Chantrea said in Khmer.

Grandma Laura laid a hand on her shoulder.

"Chantrea, we don't speak Cambodian here," she said. "While you live with me, it would be polite to use English, all right?"

"All right, Grandma Laura," Chantrea agreed.

"My wife was worried this was a government building," Grandfather said.

Uncle Bill laughed. "Nope, this is our home."

"We've lived here since Mom died," Kathy told Chantrea. "That way, my grandparents can take care of us when Dad goes on one of his business trips."

"Is he a photographer, too?" Chantrea asked as they walked toward the door.

Kathy shook her head. "No, he sells things that stores use for displays. Like mannequins and signs."

The front door opened, and a handsome man stepped out, leaning on a cane. Chantrea gasped. She had forgotten how much her grandfather looked like her father. The only differences were his gray hair and his wrinkles. But his eyes were the same sparkling hazel as Father's.

"Welcome back to Ohio, Chantrea!" he said with a broad smile.

Chantrea nodded, but did not speak.

"You've certainly grown since I saw you last," the man said.

"She's amazed at how much you look like Seth," Grandma Laura said. "Chantrea, this is your American grandfather, Grandpa Joey. Do you remember him?"

"I think so," Chantrea said. She made a little bow of respect.

"How come she bows all the time?" Jamie asked.

Kathy gave him a little shove and hushed him.

Uncle Bill introduced everyone, and they all entered the house. There was a wonderful smell in the air. Grandmother sniffed at it, a questioning look in her eyes.

"Roast beef," Grandma Laura explained.

Chantrea translated it into Khmer, then said it in English again.

"Roast beef," Grandmother said in a thick accent, as Grandpa Joey helped her out of her coat.

"You folks probably wanna freshen up a bit," he said. "Kathy, why don't you take Chantrea to your room? Meng, Teva, your room is this way . . ."

When Chantrea stepped into Kathy's room, her feet seemed to sink down a bit. She looked down and saw her new sneakers were almost buried in a blue carpet that was as thick as uncut grass. Kathy giggled at her.

"That's a shag rug," she said. "Isn't it cool?"

"Cool," Chantrea repeated.

She looked around. There were brightly colored posters all over the walls. The cover on Kathy's bed was decorated with five-petaled flowers and round yellow dots with smiling faces in the middle. The curtains on the window matched perfectly. A yellow, flower-shaped wicker lamp hung from a chain across the ceiling. Magazines with titles like *Tiger Beat* and *16* were scattered over the rug.

"Do you have one of my father's magazines?" Chantrea asked.

"Oh, no," Kathy said. "Those are news magazines. I don't read them."

"My mother had her picture in one, once," Chantrea said.

"Cool," Kathy said. She pointed to a weird, lumpy red object in one corner. "Sit down, okay? I'll get us a pop."

Chantrea lowered herself into the lump. She lost her balance and her hands and feet shot out from under her.

"It's a beanbag chair," Kathy explained.

"It's very strange," Chantrea said, gingerly sitting up.

"You'll get used to it," Kathy said. "I bet a lot of things here are odd to you."

She left and came back a moment later with two Orange Crushes. Chantrea, who did not like the beanbag chair at all, moved to sit on the desk chair. Kathy reached under her bed and pulled out a record player.

"Let's listen to some music," she said. "Did you listen to rock music in Cambodia?"

"My father liked it," Chantrea said. "So did I, and even Grandfather. Grandmother thought it was nasty."

"So do a lot of American grownups," Kathy said with a chuckle.

Kathy put a record on the turntable and turned a knob. She settled the arm over the record, and soon a song began to play. As she listened, tears began to form in Chantrea's eyes.

131

"What group is that?" she asked.

"The Eagles," Kathy replied. "It's called 'One of These Nights.' "

Now Chantrea really burst into tears.

"Hey, what's wrong?" Kathy asked. "What did I do?"

But Chantrea could not answer her. Kathy ran from the room and brought Grandma Laura back.

"What's the matter, dear?" Grandma Laura asked kindly.

"That song," Chantrea finally managed to say. "That song . . . my father really loved The Eagles. He even gave me a T-shirt once with their picture on it. It just . . . it just made me think of him. I wish he was here!"

Grandma Laura hugged her. "You poor thing. I suppose many things here will remind you of your father. But, listen to me. He *will* come back, and soon. We're doing all we can to locate him. So you must not feel sad, or worried."

She took a tissue from a box on Kathy's nightstand and handed it to Chantrea. She dried her eyes with the soft Kleenex.

"Can I see your pretty smile?"

Chantrea smiled, but just a little. That seemed to satisfy Grandma Laura.

"Dinner will be ready in twenty minutes," she said, and left the room.

"Gee," Kathy said, as she sat on the bed. "I'm real sorry."

"That's okay," Chantrea said. "We can listen to some other music."

"Did you ever hear of Linda Ronstadt?" Kathy asked.

Chantrea shook her head.

132

So Kathy played an album as Chantrea looked at the cover. *Heart Like a Wheel,* it read. Linda Ronstadt sang about someone being no good. Chantrea thought there were a lot of people she'd known in this past year who were "no good." But there were so many wonderful people, too. Especially her American family. She had forgotten they were so nice. She recalled how she'd thought they didn't like Mother, because she was Cambodian. But if that had been true once, it didn't seem true now. They were very nice to Grandmother and Grandfather. Their differences didn't seem to matter at all now. If only Mother were here to see that!

They were soon called to dinner. Chantrea thought the roast beef was the most delicious thing she'd ever eaten. Everyone was amazed to hear they rarely had meat in Cambodia, even before the Khmer Rouge.

"It was hard to get," Grandfather explained, "and expensive. We thought we were lucky when we had a chicken."

"Can we take them to the grocery this week, Dad?" Kathy asked. "I bet they'd be amazed."

Uncle Bill laughed. "I think the Moks have had enough 'culture shock' for one week, Kathy."

"What's that?" Jamie wanted to know.

"It's the strange feeling you get when you go to a new place," Grandpa Joey explained, "and everything around you is so very different from anything you've ever seen."

"It *is* different," Chantrea said, "but it's wonderful. I like it all."

"And everyone has been most kind," Grandfather added.

"Well, we're glad we've made a good impression," Grandpa Joey said. "I hope you'll always be happy here."

That night, they all gathered in the living room to watch television. Grandmother told Grandfather she thought it was magical, even though she didn't understand a word that the two young women on the screen said.

"My wife says she likes the television," Grandfather said.

"Might be a good way for her to learn English," said Grandpa Joey.

Chantrea didn't really understand a lot of the jokes herself, but she thought the things Laverne and Shirley did were very funny. She didn't remember the last time she had ever seen someone act like a clown. If there were any clowns left in Cambodia, they now planted rice in the hot sun, or dug ditches. Their smiles were forced away by the threat of guns.

At bedtime, Kathy offered to let Chantrea have her bed.

"I'll use a sleeping bag," Kathy said. "Dad says he'll get another bed soon, but I don't mind the floor for now."

"Please let me have the floor instead," Chantrea said. "The bed in the motel was too soft for me. Not very comfortable. I'm used to sleeping on a floor."

"Really?" Kathy asked. "Well, okay. But we can switch if you change your mind."

Chantrea's mind was full of thoughts as she drifted off. She thought of the many people she had left behind in Cambodia and Thailand. She thought of the new things she'd seen in the ride across America. Mostly, she thought of Father, and prayed to Buddha that tomorrow she would look out the door of the house and see him coming up the walk with his arms open to her.

But days went by, and no word about him came. On Monday, Grandma Laura announced it was time to go to school. School! Chantrea felt both excited and scared. What would it be like? Would the other children be nice, or would they make fun of her? She looked and sounded so different!

"I wish I could go with you," she told Kathy.

"I'm in high school," Kathy said, "and you're only in junior high. But it'll be okay. I'm going to walk there with you, first. Dad gave me a note in case I'm late for my own school. I'll introduce you to some of my friends' little sisters."

Chantrea went to her first day of American school dressed in a blouse made of a soft material with many different colored stripes. She wore a pair of blue corduroy slacks to match. It was one of several new outfits Grandma Laura had bought for her. Chantrea loved all the different fashions girls wore in America. They were so different from the *sampots* she wore back in Cambodia. Only the jeans and T-shirts were the same, but Grandma Laura didn't let her girls wear jeans to school.

At the school, Kathy walked with her to a group of girls.

"Hey, guys," she said.

"Hi, Kathy!" said a freckled-faced redhead. She smiled at Chantrea. "Hi, you must be Chantrea. I'm Christina, but you can call me Tina. And this is Kelly, and this is Heather."

"Hello," Chantrea said. She felt nervous and said nothing more.

"John-TREE-a," Kelly said, pronouncing the name very carefully. "That is soooo beautiful."

"Thank you," Chantrea said with a little smile.

"Tina, can you make sure Chantrea gets around okay today?" Kathy asked.

"Sure," Tina said. "We'll have a great time together."

"Don't you worry, Chantrea," Kathy said. "Dad already signed you up with the office. You just have to go to that room number on the paper Grandma Laura gave you."

They all said good-bye to Kathy, who hurried off to the high school two blocks away.

"So, do you like America?" Heather asked.

Chantrea nodded. "It's beautiful here."

She listed all the states her family had passed through on their way from California.

"Wow, you've been to nine different places!" Kelly said.

"And five different countries, too," Chantrea said, with a little pride. "Cambodia, China, Thailand, Japan and America. But we were only in China a few hours."

Her new friends agreed they had never been to so many places. Now Chantrea smiled. Imagine that she'd seen things that these American girls had never seen! She began to feel more relaxed. Tina, Kelly, and Heather were so friendly. And with her American clothes (all new, not a hand-me-down in sight), she almost looked just like every other girl. When the bell rang to signal first period, she felt very happy. She learned that she and Tina had the same homeroom.

Mrs. Beakman, the homeroom teacher, was a very pretty young woman with a warm smile. She welcomed Chantrea to America and asked the other children to welcome her, too. Almost all of Chantrea's teachers that morning were nice. And she was happy to know that Tina, Heather, and Kelly were in most of her classes.

"I think it is funny to have a different teacher for each subject," Chantrea told her new friends at lunch that day.

"Who did you like the best?" Heather asked.

"Mr. Lidle was very nice," Chantrea said. "He made me laugh. But I did not like Mrs. Baranx, our English teacher. She smiled at me, but she did not have a smile in her eyes." She shuddered.

"What's wrong, Chantrea?" Tina asked.

"It is all right," Chantrea said quickly. She had been thinking that Mrs. Baranx's smile and cold eyes were too much like the Khmer Rouge soldiers. But she did not want to spoil a great day by talking about her.

"Hey, do you like the food we have?" Kelly asked now.

"It is wonderful," Chantrea said. "So delicious."

The three girls laughed. Suddenly, Chantrea felt ashamed. Things were going to change now, weren't they? She would learn that these girls weren't nice at all. They would make fun of her and tell her to go away.

"It's okay, Chantrea, really," Tina said, as she tapped her on the arm. "We aren't laughing at *you*. We're only laughing because most of us hate this cafeteria food. I mean, what's in that stew, anyway?"

"Mystery Meat," said Heather.

Chantrea smiled again. They were not being mean to her after all. But she was amazed that they had so much food they could choose to hate any of it. If a tray like this had been given to one of the prisoners in the rice camp, that person would have thought she dined with Buddha.

"You are so lucky," she said. "You have so many things here."

Now the smiles disappeared from the other girls' faces.

"Yeah, I guess we are lucky," Heather said softly. "We learned a little about your country in social studies, Chantrea. It's a bad place, isn't it?"

"Oh, no!" Chantrea shook her head fiercely. "Cambodia is beautiful. It is the fighting that makes it bad. Do you know what? My grandparents had bananas growing near their home. And we have tigers and monkeys and so many things you only have in zoos here."

"I love monkeys," Kelly exclaimed.

Just then, a boy came over to the table. He had very straight, light blond hair and a pale face. His eyes made Chantrea think of the pale gray color of the sky just before one of the monsoon rains.

"My mom says they call kids like you half-breeds," he told Chantrea.

"Oh, Adam, get lost and stay there," Tina said crossly.

"Yeah, you big loser," said Kelly. "Leave us alone."

He paid no attention to them. He leaned closer to Chantrea. He had a terrible look on his face, as if he might hurt her. But Chantrea did not feel afraid. She stared right back at him. He was just a boy, nothing at all when compared to the Khmer Rouge soldiers.

"Go back to Vietnam, slant-eyes," he taunted.

"I am not from Vietnam," Chantrea said, her voice strong and steady.

"You're such a moron," Kelly growled. "You know she's from Cambodia."

"I know she's a dirty slant-eyes," Adam said. "And she has some nutty idea her father will come back for her. Your father ran away, girl. Don't you know that's what a lot of American soldiers do? They marry Asian women and then they leave them, 'cause they don't want to be bothered by half-breed babies like you."

"My father isn't a soldier," Chantrea said. "He's a photographer."

"Who cares what he is?" Adam sneered. "He isn't coming back for you."

"Adam Colfax, you stop that!" Tina shouted.

Suddenly, a blob of lime green Jell-O flew through the air and hit Adam in the face. Heather had shot it from her spoon. The other girls howled with laughter, but Chantrea only stared. She was too shocked by Adam's hateful words. She hardly noticed when Adam picked up a scoop of mashed potatoes from her tray and flung it at Heather.

"Food fight! Food fight!" the kids in the lunchroom began to chant.

Now Chantrea felt terrified. She ducked down and hid under the table as the other kids threw food back and forth. She heard screams, but she heard laughter, too. Why was it funny to waste food and hurt each other? she wondered. What would the people in charge do after this terrible behavior?

At last, the lunchroom monitors broke up the fight.

Tina helped Chantrea out from under the table. They dumped their trays out together and left as the bell sounded.

"Will we be in trouble?" Chantrea asked.

"Only if someone rats on someone else," Tina said. "Don't worry. If Adam says a word, I'll just tell what he said to you."

They walked down the hall. Suddenly, Chantrea was aware that some of the kids stared at her, and they didn't smile. She held her new purse close to her chest. How many others were like Adam Colfax?

She opened her locker and took out her science book.

"Tina, why is that boy Adam so mean to me?"

"Oh, he's such a turkey," Tina said. "Don't let him get to you. He's just a lot of talk, anyway. C'mon, we'll be late for science class. We have lab today, and Mr. King is so much fun."

She hurried down the hall. Chantrea ran after her. It felt as if her head was spinning. She couldn't help wondering about the terrible things that Adam had said.

In the classroom, Tina pulled her up to Mr. King, a short man with a bald head and wire-framed glasses.

"Mr. King, this is Chantrea Conway," Tina said.

"Hello, Chantrea," Mr. King said.

Chantrea started to make a bow, then remembered it wasn't the American way to say hello. She held out her hand and the science teacher shook it. He smiled at her, and welcomed her to his classroom. But she hardly heard him.

Adam's cruel words echoed in her mind. She couldn't stop thinking about her father, and wondered why it was taking him so long to contact his family.

Chapter Twelve

"CHANTREA, you seem very glum this evening," Grandma Laura said. "Didn't you have a good first day at school?"

Chantrea sat at the kitchen table, peeling apples for a pie while Grandma Laura mixed dough. Grandmother Teva sat across the table, looking at the pictures in a cookbook. She could not read the recipes, but she enjoyed the color photographs of the different American dishes.

"It was okay," Chantrea said. "One boy, he was rude to me. He called me a half-breed."

Grandma Laura clucked her tongue, making Grandmother look up. In Khmer, Grandmother asked what was wrong.

"A boy in school was rude," Chantrea said, in Khmer, too. "But it's okay. I made some nice friends, too. I don't care about him."

Grandmother nodded and went back to her reading. To be polite, Chantrea translated what she had just said for her American grandmother.

"But please don't let Grandmother know what happened," she begged. "She has been through so much and I don't want her to be hurt more."

"I understand," Grandma Laura said. "But you've been hurt enough, too. This boy—is he in any of your classes?"

"He's in my math class and my social studies class, and maybe homeroom, too, I think," Chantrea said. "Grandma Laura, why do people hate each other like that?"

Grandma Laura mixed the dough for a few moments as she thought of an answer. Then she put her spoon to the side.

"You know, Chantrea," she said, "sometimes, people act a certain way because they're afraid of something. Mostly, they're afraid of what they don't understand. I think that boy might be afraid because he doesn't understand what your life in Cambodia was like. And I think he doesn't realize that you're very much like every other kid in the world, that you aren't so different, after all."

Chantrea remembered how her mother had thought Grandma Laura and Grandpa Joey didn't like her.

"Did you think my mother was different?"

"Oh, yes," Grandma Laura said with a nod, "and I must admit I'm ashamed of the way we treated your mother at first. But we were like that boy at school—we were afraid, too. After all, an American man doesn't marry a Cambodian woman every day."

"How could you be afraid of my mother?" Chantrea asked, bewildered.

"I don't really know," Grandma Laura said. "But once we got to know her, we found out what a lovely human being she was. And we grew to love her dearly. A lot of tears were shed in this house when we got the word that she'd been killed. I'll always regret not having another chance to be with her again."

"But you have been very kind to my grandparents, and to me," Chantrea said.

"Thank you," Grandma Laura said, and picked up her spoon again. "I'll see what I can do about that boy at school. Now, how are you doing with those apples, Chantrea?"

"I'm almost finished," Chantrea said. She looked up at the clock. "When will Kathy come home?"

"In about half an hour," Grandma Laura said. "She's on the kickline team and they have practice today."

"And where is my grandfather?"

"Uncle Bill took off an extra day to show him around Columbus," Grandma Laura said. She dipped her hand into her flour canister and dusted the table with flour. Then she put the dough in the center and began to roll it.

Grandmother said something.

"Grandmother wants to know if she can roll the dough," Chantrea translated.

"Of course!" Grandma Laura said with a smile, and handed the rolling pin to the Cambodian woman.

A short time later, the pies were ready to go into the oven. When Kathy came home, she wore a blue and silver costume that Chantrea thought was very pretty. By the

143

time the others returned, too, the house smelled warmly of cinnamon and baking apples.

"Yummy!" Jamie cried as he came through the back door. He wore a baseball cap and carried a ball and mitt. "Apple pie!"

"Which you can have if you eat every bite of dinner," Uncle Bill said.

"What're we having?" Jamie asked.

"Hot dogs," Grandma Laura said. "Baked beans and salad."

"I like everything but the beans," Jamie said, "and don't put cucumbers in my salad, Grandma Laura, okay?"

Once again, Chantrea was amazed by a country where you would ever say no to food. That night at dinner, she ate three hot dogs and two helpings of salad. She felt very content when she went to bed. She said a prayer that she would hear from Father tomorrow. Then, tired after a busy day, she fell fast asleep.

When she walked with Tina into homeroom the next day, she found Mrs. Beakman decorating a bulletin board with pictures of turkeys and people who wore strange costumes.

"I know what Indians are," Chantrea said to her friend, "but who are those people in the strange hats?"

Tina laughed. "Those are Pilgrims, Chantrea. Thanksgiving is in two weeks."

Now Chantrea remembered what her father had taught her about the American holiday.

"Oh, yes," she said. "The Indians helped the Pilgrims after a long winter of hunger and sickness."

She sighed thoughtfully and stared at the bulletin board.

"Sorta like you and your family," Tina said. "You were hungry and there was sickness all around you, too. But you are safe here now. I bet you will be very thankful on Thanksgiving Day."

"Only if Father is with me," Chantrea said.

They sat down together. Adam Colfax came into the room and sneered at them.

"Flake off, Adam," Tina ordered.

She leaned forward and whispered into Chantrea's ear, "I bet if he knew what you had to go through to get here, he wouldn't be so mean."

But Chantrea wondered how Tina could possibly understand what the last months had been like for her. The American girl was nice, and maybe she would be Chantrea's best friend. But she had never worked in the hot sun, guarded by armed soldiers, while half-starved. She'd never been face-to-face with a poisonous snake.

And no one would ever shoot her mother and make her father go away.

Mrs. Beakman took attendance. The bell rang for first period, and Chantrea went to math class with Tina, Heather, and Kelly. The class had just started to learn how to make a graph. Chantrea already knew how to do that. Forty-five minutes passed quickly. English class wasn't as easy. None of Chantrea's new friends were in the class, and she hated the way Mrs. Baranx watched her all the time. She wondered if the woman thought the same way Adam did. Maybe she was afraid, too, like Grandma Laura had said. Chantrea was glad when that class was over. Social studies was much better. Mr. Lidle was really nice, and very patient when Chantrea did not understand something.

When she was in science class later that day, Mr. King divided the children into lab groups. Tina introduced her to some new friends, and Chantrea enjoyed that class best of all.

"I think almost everyone is nice," she said to her friends as they walked home.

"There are more nice people than mean people," Heather said.

"That's for sure," Tina agreed.

The next few days passed quickly. Sometimes, Chantrea felt uncomfortable because she knew people stared at her. She was the only Asian in the school and very different from the other children. But, most of the time, she was happy to be here. Tina and Heather were right—most of the kids were very friendly.

Mr. Lidle, the social studies teacher, announced a new assignment on Friday.

"This is due when you get back from vacation," he said. "That gives you well over a week to complete it."

He passed out papers to each child. To Chantrea's surprise, Mr. Lidle walked by her desk without leaving a paper. She heard moans from a few kids, but the loudest one was from Adam Colfax. Chantrea turned around to look at Tina, who sat behind her. Tina only smiled.

What was going on? she wondered.

"Class, as you can see, we're going to learn about a new country," Mr. Lidle said. "It wasn't part of my original lesson plan, but I think it would be a wonderful way to welcome Chantrea to our country if we learn about hers."

Chantrea's eyes widened. An assignment about Cambodia?

"Now, you'll see groups of names at the top of your paper," Mr. Lidle said. "Each group will research a different topic, and presentations will be made the week we get back."

"What about her?" Adam demanded. "How come she doesn't have to do anything?"

"Her name is Chantrea, Adam," Mr. Lidle reminded him. "And she does have an assignment."

He opened his desk drawer and pulled out a small blue book. When he gave it to Chantrea, the young girl noticed it had a lock on it. She had never seen a book with a lock before.

"It's a diary," Mr. Lidle said. "Chantrea, I would like for you to begin writing down your experiences."

Now Chantrea felt sad. She bowed her head.

"I don't think I can," she said quietly. "I don't want to remember the things that happened."

Mr. Lidle crouched down beside her desk. "I know it will be hard. But there is so much we don't understand about what you've been through, and I think there are children here who need to know. It was your grandma's idea. She called me. Will you try, a little? Even a few words would help us get to know you better."

Chantrea sighed. She had never backed out of an assignment in her life, and she certainly didn't want to do so in her new country. Finally, she nodded.

"I will try," she said.

"That's fine," said Mr. Lidle as he stood up. "Now, class, let's get back to the story of the Mayflower."

Later, as they walked home from school, the girls talked about their new assignment.

"I'm so glad I'm with Heather and Kelly on this," Tina exclaimed. "We're going to write about the wildlife in Cambodia."

"That will be easy," Chantrea said. "There are a lot of interesting animals."

She looked down at her books, secured with a bungee cord. The blue diary sat on top.

"I don't know if I will be able to do this," she said quietly. "To write about the past months . . . well, it would be like writing about a nightmare."

The other girls did not know what to say. They all came from comfortable homes and good families, and had never once known real fear. Finally, it was Tina who spoke.

"You know, Chantrea," she said, "sometimes, when you talk about something that scares you or makes you sad, you feel better. Maybe the diary will help you."

But for the next week, the diary sat, with blank pages, on Kathy's desk. Chantrea would look at it every day. Sometimes, she would play with the lock and key. Kathy even took out her own diary to show her.

"See, I've put some really secret stuff in here," her cousin said. "No one in the world has seen it, except for you now. Diaries are private, Chantrea. You can write anything you want, and you can show Mr. Lidle the writing. But he's a nice man, and I know he wouldn't make you read it if you don't want to."

"I just can't," Chantrea said. "When I think of those soldiers with their cold eyes, of the people with blue bags over their heads and the dead bodies . . ."

She shuddered. Kathy patted her shoulder.

"Don't think of them, then," she said. "Forget it for a while. Do you know that Thursday is Thanksgiving?"

Now Chantrea smiled. "I can't wait for my first Thanksgiving in America."

But all week long she wished and prayed that Father would be there, too. It was hard not to be disappointed when Thanksgiving Day came and there was no word at all. But everyone did their best to help keep her cheerful. They tried so hard that Chantrea finally decided to enjoy the day. Father would want her to be happy.

Dinner was delicious, and even Grandmother said so. The food was very different from anything they'd eaten in Cambodia, but the old woman was getting used to it. She was also picking up a few English phrases. She watched game shows and soap operas every day, but it was the TV commercials that helped her learn. She made everyone laugh when she sang advertising jingles.

"You're becoming a true American, Teva," Grandpa Joey teased.

Grandfather translated that into Khmer.

"Thank you, Jo-ee," Grandmother said in English.

Everyone helped clean afterwards.

"The men help as much as the women in this house," Grandma Laura said. "No escaping to the den to watch football."

Kathy held her head up high. "We're liberated here, you know."

Chantrea laughed.

"It just makes the work go faster," Uncle Bill said.

When they finished, everyone went into the den. Grandmother and Grandma Laura took out needlework. Grandmother was showing Grandma Laura how to do beautiful embroidery with silk thread. Jamie sat on the couch with Grandfather, while Uncle Bill and Grandpa Joey got comfortable in big armchairs.

"Let's go into my room," Kathy said. "I don't want to watch football."

In the bedroom, Kathy picked up a brush and a basket full of clips and elastic bands.

"Can I do a French Braid in your hair, Chantrea?" she asked. "I bet it would look pretty."

"All right," Chantrea agreed, although she didn't know what a French Braid was.

Kathy began to brush her thick black hair. She pulled hard, and soon Chantrea's scalp tingled.

"Owww!"

"My mother used to say you have to hurt to be beautiful," Kathy said.

Chantrea looked at her cousin's reflection in the vanity mirror.

"Do you miss your mother?" she asked.

"Sometimes," Kathy said. "But I only remember her a little. Jamie doesn't remember her at all."

She brushed and braided for a few more moments.

"How about you?" she asked. "Do you think of your mother?"

"All the time," Chantrea admitted.

"Was she beautiful?"

Chantrea pointed to a little box on the nightstand. Grandma Laura had given it to her, and there was only one thing inside of it. It was the wedding picture of Father and Mother, the only thing she had saved from her old life. She took it out and showed it to her cousin.

"Wow, she was very pretty," Kathy said. "And Uncle Seth looks so nice, too! Oh, Chantrea, he just has to come back for you! I know he will!"

She gave her cousin a hug, then stepped back. She held up a big mirror, and let Chantrea see the plait that ran down the back of her head.

"Oh, I like it!" Chantrea exclaimed. "When Father comes back, will you do this again so he can see?"

"You bet I will!" Kathy agreed.

There was a knock at the door. Kathy opened it to find Jamie standing there with a big grin on his face.

"What do you want, pest?"

"I wanna show you what Grandpa Meng showed me how to do!"

Before Kathy could say another word, he stepped into the room. He held out a fist and opened it to show a red paper flower.

"Watch this," he said.

He squeezed it and opened his hand again. The single red flower had turned into three smaller flowers.

"Wow!" Kathy smiled. "That was pretty good, Jamie."

"Grandpa Meng knows lots of tricks," Jamie said. "He's gonna show me."

The little boy ran off.

"Your grandfather does magic?" Kathy asked Chantrea.

"He is very good at it," Chantrea replied. "He had some fine equipment for magic back in Phnom Penh."

She thought of the intricately carved teak box where she had hidden when the soldiers first came to her city. Had someone taken that box? Or did it remain in an empty cottage, covered with a thick layer of dust?

"You've got a sad look on your face again," Kathy said. "C'mon, let's see if Grandma Laura has dessert. That should cheer you up a little!"

Grandma Laura and Grandmother had both made desserts. Chantrea and Grandfather were both delighted to see the Cambodia sweet *ansamcheks* right beside the pumpkin pie and cranberry bread. Chantrea enjoyed a little bit of everything with a big cup of hot cocoa.

That night, she was so stuffed she thought she would never want to eat again. Who would have thought, months ago in that awful rice camp, that this would be possible?

Grandma Laura came in the room to say good-night.

"I'm sorry your father wasn't here today," she said. "But there's always next Thanksgiving. I know he'll be with us by then, and you'll be surprised how fast a year can go by."

"Yes, Grandma Laura," Chantrea agreed.

Her American grandmother kissed her good-night. Kathy, who was allowed to stay up later because she was older, tiptoed into the room later on. Chantrea was still awake, and spoke in the darkness.

"Kathy, it is only one month until Christmas now, isn't it?"

"Yes," Kathy said. "Go to sleep, sweetie. It's late."

"Miracles happen at Christmas, don't they?"

"Sometimes," Kathy said.

She was silent for a few moments. Her flannel night-gown made a soft shushing sound as she dressed. Then the bed, a new one Uncle Bill had bought for Kathy, creaked a little as she climbed under the covers. Chantrea pulled up her own covers and turned on her side. She had finally gotten used to sleeping in a real bed.

"I will pray for a miracle to bring Father home to me," Chantrea said.

"So will I," Kathy promised. "But . . . you don't celebrate Christmas, do you?"

Chantrea laughed. "I celebrate all the holidays my father does, and all the ones of my Cambodian ancestors. I get twice as many holidays."

Now Kathy laughed, too. "That's nice. But we should go to sleep now. Grandma Laura says there is a big sale at Hoffer's tomorrow and she's promised to get us Christmas dresses!"

Chantrea became silent. She began to pray very, very hard that her dream to see Father by Christmas would come true. She prayed first to Buddha, and then to God. She was fast asleep before she could even finish.

Chapter Thirteen

A T breakfast the next morning, Grandpa Joey announced that he was taking Grandfather to an art supplies store.

"Turns out Meng here likes to whittle," he said. "There's a good shop near the university, and I've got some wood scraps out in the garage."

Chantrea thought of the little animals and beads her grandfather used to carve from teak. It was nice to know he would be able to do that again.

"Can I go, too, Grandpa Joey?" Jamie asked. "I don't want to go to the dumb mall with the girls."

Grandpa Joey laughed. "Sure thing."

"And maybe I will teach you how to carve," said Grandfather.

Chantrea liked the way Jamie had come to love her grandfather. Who wouldn't love him, with his magical ways and his warm smile? And Grandfather enjoyed the little boy. They had only been here a few weeks, but already it seemed they were truly part of this family. Even Grandmother seemed happy, especially when she was in the kitchen with Grandma Laura.

"Well, I've got to get the storm windows out of the garage today," Uncle Bill said. "Winter will be here before we know it, and I want them set up as soon as possible."

"Have you ever seen snow, Chantrea?" Kathy asked.

"No, not at all," Chantrea said. "Except pictures. It looks beautiful."

Uncle Bill laughed and said, "It isn't so beautiful when you have to shovel it!"

They finished breakfast, and headed out in Grandma Laura's car. On the way to the mall, Kathy tried to describe what Chantrea would see. But nothing she said prepared the Cambodians for the long stretch of stores housed under a big glass roof. For a moment, Chantrea and Grandmother simply stood at the entrance, and gazed down the long corridor.

"It is like a city!" Grandmother exclaimed.

Chantrea was too fascinated to translate. Kathy pulled her arm.

"Come on," she said. "Let's go shopping!"

Grandma Laura laughed as the girls hurried past the shops. Grandmother's head swung back and forth as she took in the fronts of each store they passed. She stopped suddenly in front of a jewelry store and admired the diamonds, rubies, and pearls in the window.

"It is like a treasure," she said.

"Grandmother said the store has treasure," Chantrea

said. "Look at the way those diamonds sparkle! My mother had a ring like that."

They went into Hoffer's Department Store. Kathy bought her clothes from the juniors department. She chose a satiny red dress with a gold belt around the middle. Chantrea was very small, and had to look in the children's section. She picked a dress of white crushed velvet with an embroidered bodice. It was so soft that she could not stop running her fingers over it, even as Grandma Laura laid it on the counter to pay for it.

"I've never had anything so beautiful," Chantrea murmured.

They looked at dresses in the women's department next.

"Tell your grandmother I would like to buy her a dress," Grandma Laura said. "As a gift."

Chantrea did so. But Grandmother shook her head.

"I do not like to wear the American kind of dress," she said. "If it would not be too much trouble, I saw a store with fabrics . . ."

"Grandma Laura?" Chantrea said.

"What, honey?"

Chantrea pressed the tips of her fingers together and made a little bow. She had not bowed like that since she first came to America, but she was about to make a big request.

"My grandmother . . . she would like to have some fabric to make her own dress."

Grandma Laura laughed. "Of course! I didn't know you could sew, Teva."

Chantrea translated. Grandmother smiled and nod-

157

ded. And so they all went to the fabric store, where Grand-mother chose a beautiful teal-colored rayon silk and some buttons and embroidery thread. They looked through pattern books until Grandmother found a simple shift that was similar to the kind of dress she might have worn back in Cambodia.

"Is anyone hungry?" Grandma Laura asked when they finished.

"I'm starved," Kathy said. "Can we get a burger?"

"We'll eat at the soda fountain in Woolworth's," Grandma Laura said.

After lunch, they headed home again. No sooner had Grandma Laura pulled into the driveway than Jamie came out, waving his arms.

"Guess what? Guess what?" he cried, as he ran up to Chantrea.

"What?" Chantrea asked. "What's happened?"

"A letter came for you today!" Jamie cried. "And it's from Thailand!"

"Thank goodness," Grandma Laura said. She pressed her hand to her chest as if her heart was beating too fast.

Chantrea hurried into the house. Her two grandfathers drank coffee at the kitchen table. Grandpa Joey read the newspaper, while Grandfather read an art magazine. They both looked up with smiles. Grandfather handed Chantrea a long white envelope.

"I hope it is good news," he said.

Chantrea's hands shook so much she could hardly open the envelope. At last, she unfolded the letter and began to read out loud:

"Dear Chantrea:

"Ever since you left us, we have been on the look-out for any word of your father. I'm happy to tell you that we have finally located him. However, I'm afraid the news is not all good."

Chantrea looked up at the adults with worried eyes. Kathy moved closer to her and put her arm around her cousin's shoulder.

"Go on," she said gently.

Chantrea took a deep breath and continued.

"I thought your father might eventually start to look around the camps here in Thailand. Even while you were still here, I had sent letters out to as many places as possible. Just last week, I finally received word from him. Chantrea, he is going to be all right. But he is in a hospital in Bangkok . . ."

Chantrea cried out. "A hospital?"

"Keep reading, Chantrea," Grandfather urged.

". . . a hospital in Bangkok. When he returned to Cambodia to find you, he started his search in Phnom Penh. Finding the city empty, he moved along the route taken by the citizens who had been forced to march to labor camps. He finally arrived at the camp where you had been interred. When they found out who he was, they became quite angry. They took everything from him, his money and his identifica-

159

tion. They tried to make him tell where you had gone. Your father managed to get away, but not before he was shot in the leg. He somehow made his way through the jungles, finding help along the way. But by the time he crossed into Thailand, the bullet wound had become severely infected. He was taken to the hospital with a high fever. It was many days before he was able to identify himself. A nurse recognized his name from my letter, and sent word to me. I went to Bangkok, where he told me this story.

"Chantrea, he misses you very much. He will soon be well, and arrangements have been made for his flight home. If all goes well, you should see him by Christmas. I'll keep you in my prayers.

"Your friend,
Jack VanBuren"

Chantrea and Kathy threw their arms around each other.

"By Christmas!" Chantrea cried. "He will be home by Christmas."

"Now we can have a wonderful holiday season," Grandma Laura said through a teary smile, "knowing Seth is on his way home."

Grandmother spoke in Khmer, "Would you tell me what the letter says? Why is everyone so happy?"

"Seth is coming home," Grandfather told her. He took the letter from Chantrea and led Grandmother into the living room. They sat on the couch together and he translated for her.

Chantrea could not stop smiling. "My dreams are finally coming true!"

That night, she finally opened the diary Mr. Lidle had given her. She had not wanted to remind herself of the things that had happened in the last months. But now that she knew Father was coming home safe and sound, she was eager to write her story. Father would want to know everything that had happened to her. And so she began to write.

She was still awake when Kathy came to bed. Her cousin pointed to the diary.

"Look how many pages you've filled," Kathy said.

"I have so much to tell," Chantrea replied. "I'm up to the part where I hunted at night with my friend Piarun. We ate raw lizards because there was no food."

"Ugh!" Kathy cried. "I wouldn't eat a raw lizard for anything."

Chantrea smiled up at her. "When you are starving, you will eat almost anything."

"I guess so," Kathy said doubtfully. "But you sure aren't going to starve here. That doesn't happen in America."

She got into her nightgown and climbed into bed.

"Chantrea, it's late," she said. "Close your journal and come to bed."

"All right," Chantrea said.

That night, for the first time in as long as she could remember, Chantrea slept soundly and peacefully.

———

ON Monday, in social studies, Chantrea told Mr. Lidle she had finally started her diary.

"That's great," Mr. Lidle said. "But what made you do it?"

Now Chantrea's smile became very big. "My father is coming home, Mr. Lidle."

"That's terrific news!" her teacher cried.

Chantrea told him all about the letter.

"And now that I know he is safe," she said when she was through, "I want to tell my story. Because I only like stories with happy endings."

Mr. Lidle gave her a hug.

"Well, this story certainly will have one," he said. "Chantrea, would you be willing to tell some of it to our class?"

Chantrea nodded. She thought of Adam Colfax, who was still nasty to her. And her new friends, who were kind, but who had never known real fear. Maybe her words would help them understand.

"Yes, I will," she said. "But not until after Father comes home, please?"

"That would be fine," Mr. Lidle said.

He called the class to order.

"Has anyone completed their assignment on Cambodia?"

A few children raised their hands. Chantrea noted they were the smartest kids, and knew they must have worked over vacation. She looked back at Adam, who stared down at his closed textbook with a scowl.

Tina's group had finished their report on animals. They got up and began to read. Tina told about tigers, bears, panthers, and monkeys. Heather read the page on herons, cranes, wild ducks, and other birds. And then Kelly told the class about king cobras, vipers, and geckos, as well as the fish that swam in the rivers.

"Very good," Mr. Lidle said. "Chantrea, have you seen many of these animals?"

"Most of them," Chantrea said. "I've seen a lot of monkeys. I heard a tiger growling once, but he was hiding in the trees. And once . . ."

She stopped. Suddenly, she felt as if she was back in the swamps, hiding in the roots of a huge banyan tree. She could hear the angry shouts of a search patrol as it hunted her down, along with the others who had escaped. She felt very hot, and her knees became all trembly. She had written about this in her diary already, and it had not bothered her then. Why now?

"Please, tell us," Mr. Lidle said in a gentle voice.

Chantrea swallowed. "It was when we had run away from the rice camp. I was hiding in the roots of a banyan tree . . ."

"What's that?" Adam interrupted.

Mr. Lidle hushed him. "Go on, Chantrea."

"The tree roots grow in the swamps. I could hear the soldiers nearby. I did not dare move, not even when a snake slithered just in front of my nose."

Someone gasped. A girl cried, "Eww! I hate snakes!"

"But it went on its way," Chantrea said. "Just like the soldiers. They went, too."

She looked around the room.

"I was afraid of the snake," she said, "and I was afraid

163

when I heard the growling tiger. But not as afraid as I was of those men."

The room was silent for a while. Even Adam had nothing to say. Finally, Mr. Lidle told the children to open their books. They began to read, but everyone was still thinking of their new classmate, hiding in a jungle full of snakes, and tigers, and men with guns.

Chapter Fourteen

CHANTREA saw her first snow a week after Jack VanBuren's letter arrived. It began to fall as she walked home with Tina, Heather, and Kelly. She became very excited, even though there were only a few flakes.

"Oh, look! It's so beautiful!" she cried. She held out her hand to catch the flakes. They melted as soon as they touched her warm palm.

"Wait until it gets really deep," Tina said. "Then we can go sledding on the hill behind the school."

"My father told me about sledding," Chantrea said. "I want my first ride to be with him."

"That'd be so neat," Heather said.

Kelly looked up at the gray sky. "It's only a light snow. You think it'll come down harder?"

"I hope so," Tina said. "Chantrea's done a lot of 'first' things lately. How about her first snow day?"

The girls all laughed, and Chantrea asked, "What's a snow day?"

"It's when you get off because the snow is too deep to go to school," Tina explained. "The buses can't run, and the teachers don't want to drive in dangerous weather."

"Oh," Chantrea said with a nod. She looked at her friends. "That's a good thing?"

"Of course it is!" Heather cried. "Who wouldn't want a day off from school?"

Chantrea thought of the months before she'd come to America, when she would have given anything to be in a classroom instead of picking rice or running through a hot, bug-infested jungle. But everyone was so happy to think about a snow day that she decided not to say anything. This was a happy moment, and there had been so few happy moments this past year.

"You want to come to my place for hot cocoa?" Kelly asked.

"I have to watch my little brother this afternoon," Heather said. "Mom's coming home late from work."

"I can come," Tina said. "How about you, Chantrea?"

Chantrea, who had grown to love hot cocoa quite a lot, thought a cup would be very nice. But what if this was the day Father called to say he was on his way home? She would feel terrible if she missed his call.

"I think I'd better go home," she said. "It's a long walk to your house, Kelly. And maybe Father will call me today."

"I think it's funny how you call him 'Father' instead of 'Dad,' " Heather said.

Chantrea shrugged. "It is just my way. I've called him that all my life."

They walked a little farther, until they reached the Conway house. Chantrea said good-bye to her friends and walked up to the door. Inside, she found her two grandmothers in the living room. Grandma Laura had a big box out, and colorful glass balls were scattered about. Grandmother held up a garland of silver tinsel, and said in Khmer how beautiful it was.

"Hello, dear," Grandma Laura said. "You're just in time to help us sort through the Christmas decorations."

"Oh, how pretty!" Chantrea said. "They are like jewels!"

Grandma Laura laughed. "Not quite so precious. But some of them are very old family heirlooms."

Chantrea picked up a little elf dressed in a green-and-red striped outfit. Its legs were tucked up inside its folded arms, and it had a pointy felt hat.

"We had one of these on our Christmas tree in Cambodia," she said.

"Yes, I sent it to your father," Grandma Laura said. "He sent me back a picture of your own Christmas tree. It was very different from the ones we have."

"We used a little palm tree in a big pot," Chantrea said. "And we hung figures that Grandfather had carved from teak with the Christmas decorations and lights that you sent us. Everyone thought it was very pretty."

Grandmother picked up a multifaceted bulb and saw her face reflected many times. She began to laugh.

"Grandmother likes your things," Chantrea said. In Khmer, she asked, "Isn't everything pretty?"

She looked at her American grandmother. "I asked if she thought it was pretty."

"Pretty, pretty," Grandmother echoed.

Jamie came in a few minutes later.

"Oh, boy!" he cried. "Christmas stuff! Did you buy my presents yet?"

"Jamie! There's more to Christmas than presents!" Grandma Laura said.

Jamie picked up something wrapped in newspaper.

"Put that down, Jamie," Grandma Laura said. "It's part of the manger. I'll be setting it up on the mantel tomorrow morning."

"Grandma Laura, can I help decorate?" Chantrea asked. "It is my first American Christmas, and tomorrow is Saturday."

"Of course you can help," Grandma Laura said.

The next afternoon, the women in the Conway house decorated the inside, while the men worked on the lights and displays outside. Grandmother tied red velvet bows on everything she could. Chantrea and Kathy decorated the banister with garland and sprays of papier-mâché fruit. Grandma Laura did the mantel. Even Jamie helped. He untangled the strings of lights that Grandpa Joey brought down from the attic. The sky grew dark early, and soon the men came through the door. A great drift of snow blew in after them.

"This is going to be some storm," Uncle Bill said. "Come on outside and have a look at the house before we're snowed in."

Everyone went out onto the snow-dusted lawn. In the

light of the street lamps, Chantrea could just barely make out strange shapes on the lawn and the roof. Grandpa Joey stood just inside the front door, his hand on a light switch.

"Are you ready?" he asked.

"Hit the lights, Dad," Uncle Bill said.

Snap! Suddenly, the whole house seemed to be encased in multicolored stars. Santa and his reindeer poised to take off from the roof. On the front lawn, life-sized figurines gathered around a manger, where a little feed trough lay empty as it waited for a special baby.

"Oh!" Chantrea cried. She could say nothing more. "Oh!"

"Isn't it cool?" Kathy said with a laugh. "Dad and our grandparents put out the best display in the neighborhood each year."

"It is like a million stars!" Grandmother cried.

Grandfather translated for everyone, and they all laughed and nodded. It did seem like a million stars. Chantrea was certain she had never seen anything so beautiful. Not even the boats that were decorated for the annual Water Festival that took place on the Tonle Sap River were this grand.

"Well, come on inside for hot cocoa and cookies," Grandma Laura said.

That night, the family gathered around the television to watch Christmas specials. Chantrea liked the story about Charlie Brown and his friends the best of all. The next afternoon, they all went Christmas shopping. Uncle Bill gave Chantrea some money to spend, and it was fun to chose things for her family. She bought a picture frame for her father.

"I'm going to have him take a picture of me," she said, "to keep inside of it."

"I think that's a great idea, Chantrea," Kathy said.

When Chantrea returned to school on Monday, the children in Mr. Lidle's class finished their reports on Cambodia. Adam Colfax had been in the group that had to report on the military. As he read about all the fighting that had plagued Cambodia over the past years, Chantrea gazed out at the snow-covered hills behind the school. How far away those soldiers and bullets seemed from this quiet little part of Columbus, Ohio.

When Adam was finished, he went back to his seat. As he passed Chantrea's desk, he asked, "How come they fight all the time in your country?"

Chantrea looked up at him. Instead of a dirty look, she saw real concern in his eyes. Maybe Mr. Lidle's project had worked, and Adam was beginning to understand what life had been like for her.

"I don't know," she said. "I don't think the adults really know, and I'm only thirteen."

"Adam, take your seat," Mr. Lidle said. "Now, I think everyone did a wonderful job on their reports. We only have one person to hear from."

He smiled at Chantrea. "But I think we can wait until after Chantrea's father comes home to hear her story. After all, what's a story without an ending?"

"What if her father doesn't come home?" someone in the back of the room whispered.

But Mr. Lidle had heard it.

"Oh, he's coming back to America," he insisted. "Don't you worry about that. I wouldn't be surprised if he's buying his airplane ticket right at this very minute!"

Chantrea grinned. Of course, it would be the middle of the night in Asia, but she knew that wouldn't stop Father. She kept that happy throught with her all the way home, and even a trip to buy the Christmas tree that night did not make her any happier.

The next day, something wonderful happened. Another letter arrived, and this time it was from Chantrea's father!

Dear Chantrea:

How wonderful it was to meet with Jack Van-Buren and learn that you are safe in Ohio! Baby, I've been looking so hard for you. I haven't stopped thinking about you for one moment in all these months. I miss you so much!

Jack told me about your mother. My heart is broken, Chantrea, to know she is gone, and to know how senseless her death was. I loved her so much.

I'm sure you want to know what has been happening with me, as I've wondered about you. We'll talk when I come home. I'm well now, and I already have my ticket to San Francisco. In fact, I'll probably be flying over the Pacific Ocean even as you read this letter!

Chantrea, I'm due to arrive in America on De-

*cember 18th. I will then take a flight to Columbus.
Hang in there, baby. We'll be together very soon!*

*Love,
Father*

Chantrea looked up at her grandmothers and her cousin Kathy, who had listened carefully as she read the letter.

"What is today's date?" she asked.

"December 16th," Kathy said. "That means your father will be in San Francisco the day after tomorrow!"

"And he'll be here the next day," Chantrea said with a smile.

Grandma Laura patted her hand. "I wouldn't be surprised if he calls you from the airport as soon as he arrives in America."

And he did! How wonderful it was to hear his voice over the phone.

"Father!" Chantrea cried. "I missed you so much! I can't wait to see you."

"I can't wait to see you, either, Chantrea," Father said. "You're gonna give me a big panda-bear hug when you see me, aren't you?"

"The biggest hug ever!" Chantrea said with a laugh. When she was a tiny girl, they called the warm, tight hugs they shared "panda-bear hugs." It would be so wonderful to feel his arms around her again.

They talked a little longer, and then Chantrea gave the phone to Grandpa Joey. He asked how Seth's flight had been, and if Seth was okay. Grandma Laura got on next and fussed over her son. There were tears in her eyes when she finally hung up.

"Thank God," she said. "Thank God he is safe and sound."

"Just one more day, and we're reunited as a family," Grandpa Joey said.

But that night, something terrible happened. A blizzard blew into Ohio. Jamie was excited to have a day off from school, but Chantrea only worried about her father.

She knelt on the living room couch with her arms folded across the back, and gazed out the window at the snow. It was so heavy she couldn't even see the house across the street. Uncle Bill came into the room and sat next to her.

"I'm afraid I have bad news, honey," Uncle Bill said.

Chantrea turned around until she sat on the soft pink cushion. She gazed at her uncle with a very serious expression. More bad news in a year of bad news, she thought.

"Columbus Airport is shut down," Uncle Bill said. "No flights in or out. You know what that means, don't you?"

Chantrea nodded her head and sighed. She knew what it meant. It meant that she would not see Father as soon as she'd expected.

Slowly, she got up from the couch and left the room. Uncle Bill called to her, but she did not answer. She went upstairs and pulled out Kathy's little record player. Soon, a song by the Eagles filled the room. Chantrea lay on her bed and just stared up at the ceiling.

Chapter Fifteen

THEY were snowed in for two days. Chantrea watched the weather report and the news, and hoped for word that the airport was open again. She didn't want to go to school, afraid she'd miss a call from her father. But, even though it was Friday, Grandma Laura insisted.

"You had two days off," she said, "and now it's time to go back."

Chantrea hardly heard her teachers that day. Her friends tried to cheer her up, but she would not laugh with them. Nothing mattered to her but seeing her father again. The Khmer Rouge had taken him away, and now the snow had done the same thing. It didn't matter that he was in America now. California was so far away he might as well be in Asia again.

She didn't say much when she walked home with her

friends. At her gate, Tina said, "I hope you hear something today."

"Thanks," Chantrea said, without smiling, as she walked up the icy path and into the house.

Her grandmothers sat at the kitchen table, drinking tea as they did every day at this time. Grandma Laura pointed to a basket of folded laundry.

"Take that upstairs when you go, will you, dear?"

"Yes, Grandma Laura," Chantrea said in a soft voice.

She saw the sad look on Grandma Laura's face, and realized that she, too, was worried. After all, Chantrea's father was Grandma Laura's own son!

Chantrea put her books on top of the clothes and lifted the basket. She walked down the hallway to the stairs. As she passed the living room, she saw someone standing there from the corner of her eye. At first, she thought it was Uncle Bill. But Uncle Bill was always at work at this hour. She turned to look.

The clothing basket tumbled to the floor.

"Father!" Chantrea cried. "Father!"

Seth Conway turned and opened his arms. Chantrea ran to him. He swung her up and around. Then put her down and covered her face with kisses.

"Look at you," he said, standing back with his hands on her arms. "Look how much you've grown!"

He pulled her close again, giving her a "panda-bear hug." "I missed you so much!"

Now the two grandmothers came into the room.

"Your father arrived here about an hour ago," Grandma Laura said. "We were all so surprised. Grandpa

Joey and Grandfather Meng are out buying another bag of rock salt. They don't even know he's here."

Chantrea smiled up at her father. He looked just as he had the day he'd left Phnom Penh back in April. Except . . .

"You have a scar on your face, Father," Chantrea said with concern.

Father touched it. "Yes, I was in a fight. But I'm all right now. Come on and sit down with me, Chantrea. I want to hear everything."

They sat on the couch together. "Father, I would rather hear what happened to you, first."

So Father told his story.

"I got word about the Khmer Rouge victory when I was in Battambang," he said. "I knew at once you were in danger, so I started back for the capital right away. But the roads were blocked by soldiers, and crowds of people. Some of my American friends warned me that we had to leave the country at once. We could be killed just for being Americans."

Chantrea looked down at her hands, folded in her lap. "They killed a lot of people, and for no good reason at all, Father."

"That's right," Father said. "I wanted to stay and look for you, but I knew if I did I might be executed."

He sighed. "I was worried something had happened to your mother, and that you would be left alone. I would be no good to you if I was dead, too. So I had to leave for a little while. But as soon as I could, I snuck back to the country. It was hard to do, but I have friends who helped me. I eventually made my way to the rice camp where you had been interred. There was a young woman there named Rann who seemed willing to help me find you."

Chantrea gasped.

"Rann tried to help you?" she asked. "She was terrible to us!"

Father shook his head.

"It was a trick," he said. "She was trying to find out where you were, so you could be arrested. I know they tried to execute you and Meng and Teva."

"A boy named Piarun helped us escape," Chantrea said.

"Where did you go next, Seth?" Grandma Laura asked.

"Someone else in the camp secretly told me of the escape," Seth replied. "I had a feeling that Meng would try to get up to Thailand, and I decided to go there myself. But by then the soldiers were demanding answers. I had to run away, and I was shot in my escape."

He rolled up his pant leg and showed Chantrea another fresh scar.

"The bullet only grazed me," he said, "but the wound got infected. I don't even remember reaching the Thai border. One day, I was on a road in Cambodia and the next thing I knew, I woke up in a hospital in Bangkok. That's where Jack VanBuren found me, and told me what had happened to you."

He smiled. "And now I'm home at last."

Chantrea hugged him. "You'll never go away again, will you?"

"No, I promise that," Father said. "I already gave notice at the magazine that I'm done taking pictures for

178

them. Instead, I'm going to see about opening up my own studio right here in Columbus."

"We'll all live here?" Chantrea asked. "I'd like that."

Father laughed. "Well, I think nine people is too many for one house. I'm going to start looking for a place for you, me, Meng, and Teva after the first of the year. Now that I'm staying in America, it's the best thing to do."

They heard the back door open, and Kathy walked in. She squealed with delight to see her uncle Seth. Jamie arrived from a friend's house a few minutes later, and shyly greeted his uncle. And the house filled with shouts of joy once again when Uncle Bill and Grandpa Joey returned.

The dinner they shared that night was the happiest ever. Seth had surprised his family with his arrival, so Grandma Laura did not have anything special to cook. But the spaghetti and meatballs were as wonderful as any fancy dish. The table was so full of conversation that they hardly tasted their food.

"Chantrea, I want to hear about you, too," Father said.

Chantrea asked Grandma Laura if she could leave the table for a moment. Then she hurried upstairs and got the journal. She brought it back to the dining room and handed it to her father.

"I wrote everything down that I could remember," she said. "Even the bad things. Now I can write happy things, too!"

Father looked down at the diary as if it was the most precious book in the world.

"I'm going to read this very carefully," he said.

T HE next morning, when he came down to breakfast he looked very tired. He rubbed his eyes and yawned as Grandma Laura set a plate of muffins and a cup of coffee in front of him.

"Father, are you all right?" Chantrea asked with worry in her voice.

He smiled. "I was up very late. I couldn't stop reading your journal. All the terrible things that happened to you"—he paused and shook his head—"Chantrea, no child should see the things you have seen. You're a very strong and special girl, do you know that?"

They embraced. Chantrea was certain she would never get tired of hugging him.

"I'm not so special," Chantrea insisted. "I'm only one of many."

"I keep thinking of your mother," Father said, "and how she sacrificed her life to save you. She was a beautiful, remarkable woman."

"I know, Father," Chantrea said softly. For a moment, they just gazed at each other, both filled with thoughts of beautiful Dara. Then Father turned to Grandfather.

"I'm amazed at what you did to save the family, Meng," Father said. "I don't think I would even have thought of building a raft!"

Grandfather nodded. "It does seem like it was a bad dream, Seth. I still have nightmares about those months. I think that Teva does, too. But she does not ever talk about it."

"I don't blame her," Father said. "But I also hope that she tells her story, too, someday. That you both do. People should know what is happening in that country."

"Cambodia is a sad place now," Meng agreed.

Grandma Laura refilled the coffee cups and milk glasses.

"But America is a happy place," she reminded them, "and you are here as long as you want to stay."

Grandfather nodded. "Yes, soon we will study to become citizens."

"It's Saturday," Father said. "What do you want to do, Chantrea? Anything, anything at all."

Chantrea thought for a moment. Then she grinned.

"I want to have a game of catch," she said.

"Catch?" Jamie echoed. "In the snow? Who plays catch in the snow?"

Kathy gave him a poke to quiet him.

"We can do that," Father said, smiling at Chantrea. "In fact, I've got something we can use that's very special."

He got up and left the room. Soon, he came back with a small square box.

"Remember the day I left Phnom Penh?" he asked. "I said I would bring you back a surprise."

"Oh, yes!" Chantrea said.

"Well, here it is," Father told her, and gave her the box.

Chantrea opened it to find a baseball, covered with writing.

"I had written to my boss here in Columbus and said how much we liked the Cincinnati Reds," Father explained. "He got this ball signed for you by different members of the team, and brought it to Cambodia when he came to do some of his own work. I had planned to bring it back to Phnom Penh after my assignment was done."

He sighed. "I never thought I'd have a chance to give it to you."

"It's wonderful, Father," Chantrea said. "Thank you! But . . . it's so special. I don't want the snow to ruin it."

"Jamie has a lot of baseballs," Grandma Laura said. "You can use one of those."

"And who knows what you'll find under the Christmas tree?" Father said. "I think you need all kinds of baseball equipment."

Kathy laughed. "You should go out for the school baseball team in the spring, Chantrea. You might just be the first girl member!"

"I wouldn't be surprised," Father said.

Chantrea could not stop smiling. Her family was safe and sound at last. Father was home, never to go away again.

She knew there would be a lot of games of catch in the future.

Author's Note
Chantrea Conway's Story

AFTER the Nazis killed ten million people, including six million Jews, in World War II, many people vowed "never again." Sadly, the cruelty of dictators such as Adolph Hitler remains with us. Pol Pot, a leader of Cambodia in the 1970s, was one such dictator. It is estimated that during his reign some three million people died from disease, starvation, overwork, or execution.

Pol Pot believed that many of Cambodia's problems came from being under foreign rule throughout its history. His solution was to start all over again, as if the country had no past. He declared 1975 the "Year Zero." Under threat from the Khmer Rouge (Cambodian Communist) army, entire cities were evacuated. The people were driven to march for days, until they died or were forced into slave labor. Everyone had to leave their old lives behind, and become farmers. Young children were separated from their parents and sent to special schools to learn the ways of the Khmer Rouge.

Anyone who questioned the ways of the Khmer Rouge committee, known as "Angkar," was executed. A person could be killed for the slightest disobedience, even for speaking a foreign language. No one really knows how many people were taken from prisons and slave camps to be executed. The site of their deaths, where countless skeletons have been found, became known as "The Killing Fields."

Pol Pot's nightmare reign lasted from 1975 until 1979, when he was forced out by invading Vietnamese troops. He wasn't arrested for his role in the genocide until 1997. He died in April of 1998, twenty-three years after the fall of Phnom Penh.